PRAISE...

"I first read Mary's stories a few years ago in a critique group, in the UK, where we strive to help each other better the writing. Not that we were able to help Mary — we got too caught up in the delightful tales. Her charming characters warmed our hearts, her exotic settings awed our minds, and her deft appreciation for humanity left us wanting more.

"Mary's Hong Kong stories shine on a colonial time and place few truly knew. These short tales are complete in themselves, and together weave a delightful tapestry of a place and people after the resumption of British sovereignty once the Japanese occupation ended with WWII.

"Her father worked for the British Hong Kong Government and embraced the city, teaching his children to do the same. These are astonishing vignettes of a childhood adventure far from ordinary."

Jo Sparkes

Her awards include the Kay Snow for best screenplay, three B.R.A.G. Medallions, and a silver IPPY. Latest book The Honey Trail published in December 2023

I

II

HONG KONG

Memories, Stories & Anecdotes from My Colonial Childhood 1955 to 1968

Mary Levycky

Tim Saunders Publications

TS

Tim Saunders Publications

Copyright © 2023 Mary Levycky

All rights reserved

The events portrayed actually happened and the author
has written them as she personally remembers them as
a child; childhood memories are not guaranteed to be
accurate. They may not be remembered by others exactly
as the author does. Other than my family, the names of
most people have been changed to assure their privacy
including my amah whom I've called Ah Chun.

Cover photograph: My mother and her father on a
Sampan - my dad is on the left. I like the wave of their
hands!
Cover design: Mark Norton
(mark.diamondg@gmail.com) and Mary Levycky

CONTENTS

INTRODUCTION

This collection of stories about my life growing up in Hong Kong in the 1950s and 1960s was initially instigated by my niece, Claire, asking me questions about my childhood. Writing to her brought it home to me, sadly, that my era was now long gone, just like so many of the protagonists in these stories; my mother and father and all their friends, my grandparents and many others - and I myself will surely follow suit in the not too distant future! I realised that if my life during these years remained unrecorded it would be as if it had never existed, and an entire world in which I and so many had flourished and developed could disappear just like dust in the wind.

Background
Hong Kong Chinese, Hongkongers, and those from the mainland are ethnically similar but their backgrounds are very different. Over the generations their upbringing has influenced their attitudes and beliefs. Hongkongers are the offspring of parents and grandparents who rejected the Chinese Communist Party, Mao Tse-tung, his Gang of Four and the murderous Red Guards. They refused to engage with

the persecution and killing of the educated, intelligentsia, teachers and thinkers and the spiritual or religious, be they holders of the two-and-a-half thousand year old traditional Confucian ethos or were Taoist, Buddhist, or Christians. Because in common with Soviet and other forms of Communism all spiritual belief was forbidden and only the party could be worshipped. Those whose lives included teachings on how to live with kindness and humanity were forced to deny their faiths or flee, mainly to Hong Kong.

Many of these anti-communists built temples, churches, mosques, synagogues and more. They upheld the idea of a civil, fair and kindly society, the antipathy in fact from that which they had fled. They regarded the massacre of those left behind in China with grief and loathing; forty million had been slaughtered. In Hong Kong they lived a peaceful life - in spite of agitators from Communist China - and they helped build the success of the place they now called home.

Our lives were cradled in the care of these Hongkongers. We children were always looked after by adults whose attitude was old-fashioned. That is, they believed that all children were the responsibility of all adults. We roamed far and wide safely, knowing if we had a problem we could ask for help and it would be immediately forthcoming - and we did, and it was. This was still true in the ten years of my life with my own children in Hong Kong during the 1970s and 1980s; they too were cared for - I could sunbathe undisturbed while laughing young office workers played games and built sandcastles, unasked, with my little boys.

The idea of Hong Kong, against the "in perpetuity" terms of the Treaty of Nanking of 1842, being surrendered to China in 1997 was obviously horrific to so many. One child Chinese from the mainland, having grown up without any siblings or spiritual dimension, had become selfish, uncivilised and indulged, as Hongkongers discovered once mainlanders were allowed to cross the border! For instance, guards had to be put around buffets in hotels because mainlanders would come and take all the food. Rules about numbers of unruly mainlanders in any one place had to be instituted. Chinese tourists had to be trained about how to behave abroad. Thousands of years of civilisation in one of the oldest countries in the world had been destroyed.

But in our time there was peace, freedom of belief, expression and employment, music (much of which involved my father), festivals, security, law and order. One of the most generous charities in the world is Hong Kong's Community Chest, famously assisting over one-and-a-half million from a population of eight million - those who are most in need generously supported by those with enough.

My memories here are subjective of course. I am writing about events sixty-five years ago and my personal memories will not be as others necessarily saw them! But I sincerely hope that many of these stories reflect the optimism and vitality of living in Hong Kong during that wonderful era.

Mary Levycky
November 2023

DEDICATION

Dedicated to the memory of my wonderful parents, Harold and Thelma Miller.
And to my patient husband Tony Levycky - thank you!

FAREWELL ENGLAND

A photo of the family in 1957. We were aged ten, six and two at the time.

One afternoon Dad came home from the office and announced that he thought we should go abroad to live. He said he was tired of driving up to London and working five-and-a-half days a week and only seeing his children in the very early mornings before he left and rushing home in time to kiss us goodnight. At the time I was seven-and-a-half, Trudi was four and Sally was a couple of months old.

We children of course couldn't conceive of this, but Dad had already been to The Royal Institution of Chartered Surveyors to see if there was a suitable job in the sunshine. When he came home that evening he got the atlas out and showed us the two places where there were available positions – Trinidad and Hong Kong. Knowing nothing about either, Mum asked which would be the most interesting job and he replied, probably Hong Kong.

We all stared at the map. Well, not Sally of course because she had just been fed and was asleep on Mum's lap, but the rest of us did. Dad showed us a tiny dot on the other side of the world.

"That's a long way away, Harold," said Mum.

"It will be very exciting!" Dad replied.

Mother trying to digest the fact that she was leaving to go to Hong Kong imminently.

"So when would we leave?" she asked hesitantly, gazing out at the green fields and huge chestnut trees in the Kent countryside she loved so much, her blue eyes wide while she absorbed the information that we would leave as soon as possible, because if he got the job it started right away. And of course, he did get the job. As this was sixty-eight years ago I consider it brave of our mother to be willing to gather her children and set off into the blue - not a lot of people did that then.

A few days later a very posh lady from the colonial Women's Corona Society of Hong Kong came to tea. Dressed in a pretty frock Mum had made for me, I passed around the sandwiches. The summer sun slanted through our cottage window onto Dad's grand piano, which was standing alone in its own small extension, on the plinth Dad had built for it. It had once belonged to Gracie Fields[1] and was a beautiful small walnut grand. I remember wondering how they could get it onto a boat - the answer was, they didn't, it went into storage, but Dad had it until the day he died when he was ninety-one and actually recorded his final CD on it at that ripe old age.

The Corona Society lady (she was actually Lady somebody) droned on about how Mum would have to employ a baby amah[2] and also a cook amah in Hong Kong. This person would apparently follow her around at the market and carry her multitudinous purchases. How extraordinary this seemed to Mother! We were still severely rationed in England in the mid fifties after the war, and certainly she had never envisaged walking around foreign markets buying unknown exotica to be carried by a servant trailing along behind her.

It was difficult enough to feed us at the time as it was and we lived largely on rabbits from the farmer down the road, who often shot them because they ate his vegetables and who frequently brought a brace of them to Mum in humble worship of her beauty. We thrived on rabbit stew, rabbit pie, rabbit and dumplings... Dad grew vegetables and we children had our own spades to dig up carrots and potatoes. In the garden we had red and white currants, blackberries, apples and pears. What more could we want?

Our parents had a reason to leave unfortunately, because of my whooping cough, which had developed into asthma. I was missing lots of school, and Trudi tells me it was very unsettling for her to wake in the morning and find an ambulance had spirited me away in the night to hospital. The doctor told our parents that the weather was making my condition worse and that they should find a warmer climate for me – well, Hong Kong was most certainly hotter than Westerham, Kent.

Dad's mother Lydia, our Nana, came to help pack up the cottage. I don't remember much about this because I spent most of the time banished outdoors to play with my little sister Trudi, where we made tents of white sheets while the baby slept in her big blue pram in the garden. Sally was a very good baby, possibly because she was born in lovely sunshine and before she knew anything was plunged into the stimulation of all sorts of dramas and excitements with people rushing about. I remember it was a beautiful summer.

Father decided we had to leave in style. I didn't realise it then but he was a showman at heart, so he booked Sir Winston Churchill's Rolls Royce and chauffeur to drive us in flagrant luxury to Southampton to catch the P&O ship, the M/S Carthage, for the six week trip to Hong Kong. The car and chauffeur were available if Sir Winston wasn't at Chartwell, his house in Westerham. Everyone, even Churchill's chauffeur, had to make a bit extra in those days.

Something I should mention is that our parents were notoriously late. Dad timed everything down to the last minute. We have missed planes because of this - most noticeably when we missed the flight from Los Angeles to Mexico because Dad decided we had time to drive down to Ocean World and back, which it turned out we didn't. But I digress.

Eventually we loaded all our bags and suitcases into the boot, and I was squashed into the back seat with Nana, Trudi and Mum cradling baby Sally, while in front Dad urged the chauffeur on with increasing panic. The chauffeur was unmoved however, saying, "Mr Miller, this is Sir Winston's car, we don't take her over twenty miles an hour." Dad's mother, Nana, sitting next to me, repeatedly suggested that Dad calmed down, while Mum rocked her baby and stared out of the window. I couldn't see a thing because I was sitting behind the chauffeur's hat, but I do remember the sedate and seemingly endless drive, and Dad frequently turning round from the front seat and asking, "Are you all right, Mother?"

I remember the chaos at the dock, the immense size of the ship, the noise and Nana in her blue tweed coat, which she later cut up to make two coats with blue velvet collars for Trudi and me. I think Sally may even have worn one of them eventually. Then we climbed up the gangway with me carrying my teddy, which I still have.

The smell of wood, tar and salt that first assailed you as you boarded a liner in the 1950s is unforgettable. On the deck stood lines of people holding multi-coloured paper streamers, which were caught and held by their loved ones on the shore. Nana stood there all alone, holding ours. Then the band struck up and, to the sound of music and cheering and the sobs of the people on the deck, the ship blew her three deep blasts as we slowly drew away from land, the streamers snapping and drifting into the sea as we went.

Although we repeated this exercise a number of times over the years, I recall this first time vividly. Perhaps it was the sight of Nana standing there all by herself in the chilly, sunless evening.

After setting sail we walked down the sweeping curved staircase to our cabins. In ours we children had two bunk beds and a cot for Sally. Mum and Dad had the adjoining cabin next door. Although it was first class accommodation it was certainly not roomy or generous! Of course there was no air-conditioning but we had blowers, which were brass, ball-shaped things built into the wood-panelled walls, which you could twist to blow air in whichever direction you chose.

The smell of a liner in those days was totally idiosyncratic. The corridor floors were covered in shiny, polished, deep red or dark green linoleum. The walls were wood-panelled and the highly polished wooden handrails smelt of beeswax. There was a lot of coir matting at doors, which has a unique smell, now as then, especially when it is damp as it was generally. In the bathrooms there were huge baths, which featured boiling hot seawater - that is definitely a smell you never forget! Nor the steamy atmosphere, and to top it off the oblong cedar floor mats, which were usually wet and very big to stop people slipping, and which had a pungent and indescribably nice odour.

However, once we got into the Bay of Biscay

things took a turn for the worse, when both our parents succumbed to seasickness. I remember Mother feeding the baby whilst bent over the sink trying to wash out our sheets, and the two of them trying to look after us while feeling as if they were about to collapse and die.

Personally, I don't remember being seasick and I've have never been seasick since but Trudi assures me we both were. I certainly remember Mum in our cabin throwing up while the baby howled. "How revolting," is all I can say looking back, "to sail away into the unknown in a miasma of nausea!"

First Class is not the best fun for children, I feel. There were very few of us, probably half a dozen. The grown-ups had a lovely time; every evening there were dances, games, quizzes, faux horse-racing and other events after a sumptuous five course meal. For us, there was a children's supper at half past five in a corner of the dining room where we had extraordinary foreign food such as spaghetti bolognese. Sally was just big enough to be propped up on pillows in a high chair and she had runny cereal called Farex for her supper, like all English babies in those days. She graduated to a Farley's rusk, which she shoved into her mouth with both hands. The rusk squeezed through her fingers and dropped onto the high chair's table, whereupon she threw it into my long hair with gay abandon, where it stuck.

I discovered there was a small gate to the left of the First Class bar on the swimming pool deck. Beyond it, down the steps, lay the glories of Second Class. Oh how I yearned to be Second Class! Children were running about, there was music, children were playing games and having a wonderful time. As we approached the Middle East the swimming pool was filled up and children were jumping in and splashing each other – Trudi and I sneaked through the gate and joined in.

We were discovered of course and ushered back to the elegant, gin-and-tonic First Class deck. There, slender gentlemen languidly chatted up ladies in flowery swimsuits (including Mother). We sat on the deck beside her, crossed-legged, with our books while bow-tied waiters whisked around us carrying trays of fancy drinks flaunting pineapple chunks, maraschino cherries and mini umbrellas. Soft music played.

Down in Second Class, meanwhile, hairy chested fathers with tattoos and big bellies laughed as they threw balls and children into the pool amongst shrieks of joy. Oh, wouldn't anyone long to be Second Class? Though not Mum and Dad I suppose because they were having a ball with one event after another. One night they went to a fancy dress party where they had to wear a hat that illustrated a piece of music. I thought Mum's was genius; they half inflated Sally's big rubber duck so it was flopping about disconsolately on Mum's head, with a label saying "The Dying Swan". I couldn't stop laughing.

The swimming pools were filled from the sea. The water differs from ocean to ocean – the Atlantic looks, tastes and smells different from the Indian Ocean, which is my favourite sea, green and soft. The ship pulled into Aden at the start of the Suez Canal, which in those days was dusty desert with camels outlined against the sky as they walked along the canal's edge, palm trees in the background. The ship proceeded along the canal at a couple of knots, slow enough to allow hordes of lads to shin up the sides of the ship on ropes, bringing with them goods to sell. They laid them out along the deck on squares of red cloth: leather items of all sorts, purses, patched leather camel stools with folding wooden stands, handbags, belts.

Then the gully-gully man arrived. Gully-gully men were magicians and all the children on board sat on the deck and watched with the adults standing behind them, as the gully-gully man magicked chicks from ears and noses, threw watches into the sea only to miraculously find them again behind somebody's ear... it was all very mysterious. They tied their little boats to the side of the ship, then after a time, they descended their ropes with their articles of magic and their earnings to wait for another. The banks of the narrow canal slid by as we moved noiselessly along.

We went to Ceylon where we developed a taste for mangoes never to be overturned, and then we arrived in Bombay. At that time passenger ships anchored in the harbour and small, shiny white tenders came and collected the passengers to go to shore. Mum dressed Trudi and me in blue striped sundresses she had made for us, and off we went to look for baby food, Sally in her folding pushchair. I remember the wide avenues, the trees, the people, the smells that I still love and did then even at that age – sandalwood, vanilla, rosewater, cedar. I have a memory of standing in a large emporium with Mum politely asking for (non-existent) baby food, while a smooth talking Indian salesman did his best to sell her silk dressing gowns and jewels instead.

Eventually, we pulled into Hong Kong harbour for the very first time. It was busy, full of sampans$_3$, junks$_4$ and the iconic, green Star Ferries with their white roofs. There were ships of all shapes and sizes. It was about twice as wide then as it has now become due to reclamation. The mountains on either side of the harbour loomed above us, and on Kowloon Pier the band played to greet us as we gently drew alongside.

I would be misleading you if I said I could remember everything about our arrival because it was all a chaotic jumble. We were taken to a hotel in Kowloon where we stayed for a month or two. Dad's new boss, Fred, collected us the day after we arrived and drove us up to the top of Kowloon Peak, from where we gazed out for the first time at the lights of the harbour, which were to become so familiar and precious to us.

It was obvious to Dad that the first thing we had to do was get a car. A couple of days after that, Dad by chance, typically, met a man on the ferry who wanted to sell his Jaguar Mark V, a superb luxury car that everybody, especially Dad, fell in love with. *She* (Dad always referred to it as *she*) was a big, silver-grey machine with running boards, a leaping jaguar on the long bonnet and a sexy curved up back. It had a walnut dashboard, a sliding panel on the roof and grey leather seats. Dad loved it as no other car and we had it for a long time; a double-edged joy because in the summer heat the smell of leather was asphyxiating, the wood absorbed Mother's expensive perfume, which was totally overpowering and you could hardly sit on the scorching leather seats.

But still, it looked wonderful and it played a major role in our lives - until one fateful day, years later, Dad's pride and joy died of a broken back axle in the outside lane of the packed main road roundabout leading towards the Peak at rush hour, when Mother happened to be driving on her own. The car blocked the entire road as every following car tried to get into the inside lane to pass it, but the Jag was immovable. Then it started raining so Mother was standing helplessly in the middle of Garden Road soaking wet, waiting and hoping for the police to bring some sort of tow truck while people all around her were relentlessly manoeuvring and hooting. It was all an inconceivable trauma! And a fittingly dramatic finale for an adored Jaguar Queen.

This is the famous Jaguar Mark V with Mum and Ah Tai, our first amah, holding Sally

ON TYPHOONS, AMAHS AND AH CHUN

A typhoon had hit Hong Kong like a volcanic explosion leaving the usual mess; ships blown onto shore, landslides, roads blocked, smashed and washed up cars, trees upended, general chaos and all of it overlaid with the stench of rotting vegetation steaming in the sun.

We arrived in Hong Kong in late September, and although we had just missed her, the typhoon had a considerable influence on where my parents decided we would live because of the powerful effect it had on the weather. It was unbelievably humid. Water dripped off our fringes and down our noses. It was so incredibly hot that although we had just spent over six weeks on board the SS Carthage and travelled through the Suez Canal, had three days in Bombay and a further few in Singapore, nothing struck us as nearly as hot as Hong Kong.

We were booked into an old, colonial hotel halfway up Nathan Road in Kowloon. It was quaint and charming in its way; lush internal gardens had open verandahs from each room with little stone paths to the goldfish ponds in the centre. Hibiscus hedges full of red flowers surrounded and protected the pretty gardens.

There was a very colonial-style restaurant which wouldn't have been out of place in Worthing in 1925, with white damask tablecloths and gloved waiters serving brown Windsor soup and roasts. I recall the curious beef sausages which we had for breakfast, triangular in shape because they came squashed up from a tin and which I grew to love. Chicken livers in madeira on toast was another of my favourites. It was all very peaceful.

However, it didn't remain so for long. Things livened up a few days after our arrival when there was a flying ant swarm. Their wings dropped like snow and piled up in the corners. The air was dense with thousands of them and we were all disgusted and terrified. I remember the staff racing around trying to hoover them up or somehow bat them away while we cowered in our rooms with the doors closed. Wingless and revolting, they crawled under the doors and through the window frames.

To top it off, the humidity gave me an asthma attack and I was carted off by ambulance to Kowloon Hospital, so that was that. We were not, my parents vowed, living downtown - and especially not anywhere near Nathan Road, Kowloon.

Since Father had collected his wonderful car from the man he had met on the Star Ferry, we travelled in this vehicle of delight to find a more salubrious environment. Mother fell in love with Victoria Peak. In those days it seemed quite remote, green and cool. It was surrounded by mist for about three months of the year, like Sintra in Portugal, but that didn't bother Mum. All she wanted was to get as far away as possible from Nathan Road.

In fact in twenty years she never changed. My sister Trudi and I went to senior school in Kowloon, beyond Kai Tak airport every day, all the way from the Peak. If Mother was planning to go though, she would sigh and tell us on Monday in a doom-filled voice that she was "going to Kowloon on Thursday," usually with her great friend Auntie Mary, as if it was Timbuktu. When the two of them got off the ferry, before anything else they would have to sit down in the plush surroundings of the Peninsula Hotel for a reviving tea and some tiny little sandwiches to adjust to the shock.

Before we left England, Mother had been advised that she would need domestic help, which she thought absurd. However, once in Hong Kong, the shopping, cooking and household running was completely foreign to her – the thought of ordering our supply of food and goods to be delivered from Charn Kee the compradore$_5$ (this was well before supermarkets were dreamt of) initially bewildered her. As for going to the crazy, busy markets with their lumps of unrecognisable meat on hooks, the unknown fish, the noise and shouting and the raw smell of everything, she found she could not do on her own with a baby. She hired a sweet country girl who spoke a little pidgin English, called Ah Tai. Soon Ah Tai, with baby sister Sally on her back, was trotting Mother around the markets and buying what we needed.

When a flat in Peak Mansions at the top of the Peak became available we moved in and were home. The flat was far too big for Ah Tai to manage so Mother found a young couple who needed an amah and Ah Tai moved to help them - apparently they were thrilled because Mum had taught Ah Tai to make such delicacies as bread and butter pudding. Then Mother advertised for an amah duo, as was normal at that time.

Amahs in the Far East, although seeming to have much in common with traditional ayahs in colonial India, came from a different background. In India an ayah would be a children's nurse, not expected to cook or clean as she would be of a higher caste than the cleaning wallahs, for instance the dhobi wallah, the washerman.

The background of Chinese amahs working in the Far East though was one of liberation and emancipation on the part of illiterate young, Cantonese country women who came from a specific area, the Pearl River delta in Guangdong. Chinese women generally were adjuncts of men and unbelievably now, it was forbidden by law to pay them directly. They worked beside the men as well as doing the cooking, cleaning and childcare but no money or reward could ever touch their hands and what they received depended entirely on their husbands.

Once women saw that it was possible to work for themselves in Hong Kong, Singapore or in Shanghai until 1940 when the British left, and to be paid with money in their own right, they established a sister society with simple rules. These were to commit to a chaste life, to work and support each other, usually working in pairs, to work for themselves without any man controlling them, to contribute to housing for elderly members of the society and to be free to accept or leave any employment. They usually worked for the same family for several generations and became devoted to their adopted family, showing a kind of altruism that is almost unimaginable these days. In return the family would expect to support them in their retirement.

Their uniform was a pair of loose black trousers and a white, long sleeved cotton top buttoned to the side with coiled cloth buttons. Younger amahs wore their hair in a long plait down their back. Older women would put it in a bun in the nape of their neck. Having long hair was, interestingly, an act of defiance because when the Manchu Qing dynasty conquered the Han Chinese they ruled that hair should be cut. Han Chinese could be executed if they disobeyed, which they did because their belief was that their hair and their body were gifts from their parents to them and shouldn't be tampered with. The Qing dynasty was overthrown in 1912 but Hong Kong rebels are still calling themselves Long Hairs even today. And amahs kept their hair long.

Mother searched around for an amah duo with a good reputation, and thank goodness one day she found one when Ah Chun arrived. Ah Chun became the background to our lives as we grew up, Mother's right hand woman. She did the cooking, and Ah Oi did the washing, and together they did the housework in the mornings. They rested in the afternoons, before Ah Chun started cooking supper and Ah Oi did the ironing, listening to screeching Chinese opera on the radio with her neighbours. They had their own rooms, balcony, kitchen and bathroom. The form of address from Amah to employer was "Missie" and "Master".

To give Ah Chun her due I would have to write a book just about her many years with us. Her signature good morning to me was when she got me up for school. "Ma Lai you get up now you velly late!" I can hear her now. She was thoughtful, for instance she always had cold rice in the fridge because my little sister Sally liked to sit on the kitchen step with her and eat a bowl of rice when she came home from school. She made me, on the other hand, two chocolate cakes a week because when I finally reached home after my laborious journey from school and before I slumped on the floor for my hour long telephone call session, I had to have a large slice of that particular cake made by her. Nothing else would do.

Ah Chun did have some old fashioned ideas. For instance, one day she sat down next to me on my bed, looking serious.

"Now you sixteen, you grow up," she stated. I wondered what she was going to say next.

"Now you grow up, I call you Young Missee."

"No!" I cried.

"Yes," she said firmly.

"I won't answer you if you call me Young Missie!"

"Must be," she said uncompromisingly.

"No. You can't!"

She stood up, disappointed in me. I think she fancied the idea. However, the thought died a death because Mum told her that I didn't want her to and the next morning, *bang* went the door, and "Ma Lai, you get up now..!" bellowed Ah Chun.

Every few months Ah Chun and Ah Oi, and intermittently a young, trainee amah who was called a "makee-learn" would strip the wax off the beautiful parquet floor with fine steel wool. They spent hours rubbing the floor with this wool with their feet in their black plastic shoes. The following day they would spread new wax polish over it. Then came the bumper[6]. It was a very heavy, oblong, steel object shaped like a fat book, with a sliding connection on top attached to a wooden pole with which you pushed and pulled, it had a dark red felt underside. It had a momentum of its own - click clack, click clack it went as it slid back and forth over the floor to shine the wax. I found this sound soporific, and as they started very early in the morning the reassuring sound of the bumper told me as I dozed that Ah Chun was there and all was well.

The events of our lives over the years were inevitably entwined with Ah Chun but one day this came to an abrupt end. I came home from school and found her talking with Mum and Dad in the dining room, in tears. I opened my mouth to speak but was told to go away. Ah Chun had a letter in her hands and Mum sounded distressed, saying no, over and over again. But no matter what they said, Ah Chun seemed determined. Later they told me what was happening. When Ah Chun had left China, an elderly auntie had remained in the Chun village house to maintain a Chun presence, as most families tried to do. However, this house had been taken over by the Red Guards and the auntie had been taken off to a commune to work.

Communist Chinese then believed people were disposable pawns, their value based only on how much work they could do. Auntie had written to tell Ah Chun that she was not able to do the work required of her any more owing to her painful hip, broken wrist (which they had refused to set) and her arthritis. Therefore, the commune leaders demanded that her niece return to China and take her auntie's place working on the commune. To that end, they were making the auntie kneel on broken glass for hours on end until she was replaced by Ah Chun.

There was nothing we could say or do, no tears or reasoning, no strings Dad could pull, because in the end, inevitably, Ah Chun went. She sewed money into her clothing and took whatever we could think of for her to take but in our hearts we knew they would search her and find it all. I don't know how she got back into China. The three of them left in the car a couple of days later. Presumably, Mum and Dad drove her as near to the border as they could. I felt lost, it was bizarre without her, part of us was missing.

Ah Chun never returned. We had one letter from her to say that her auntie had died from her wounds, and that she would have to remain in China "for a few weeks". Week after week went by with no contact. We grew very anxious; Dad asked his friend in Immigration to try and find out anything he could through any covert contacts he had but they drew a blank. Mum and Dad explored every possible avenue. We never had another letter. Ah Oi didn't have the heart to work without her partner. Soon, tearfully, she left us to go to the community house. She was elderly and illiterate and unless she phoned us, we couldn't keep in touch with her. We knew if she needed more money or had other problems it was not a question of whether she could get in touch with us because of course she had our address and phone number, but of whether she would – and she never did. Possibly she herself even went to China to look for Ah Chun, because this was something she said she might do.

But as it was, Ah Chun was gone without trace, as if the earth had swallowed her up. For over three years Mum and Dad tried to find her. It was impossible. We presume she may have been killed. And if so, Rest in Peace, our dear and never forgotten friend.

GRANDAD AND THE LEPER ISLAND
- HEI LING CHAU

Grandad and the leper island. This is Hei Ling Chau. Back row: Nana, me, Granny and Mum. Front row: Trudi, Grandad and Sally. The little pier in the background.

Our grandfather, Sidney was an altogether larger than life character. He came to join us in Hong Kong from India, where he had been living on top of a mountain in the Hindu Kush with his friend, Robbie Robinson. They were twenty years in advance of The Beatles in discovering Hindu spiritualism and Ravi Shankar, chanting mantras and seeking for the transcendental meaning of life. Grandad had been deeply interested in the spiritual life well before decamping to India however, as a leading light in the Theosophical movement in London and around the country.

Before moving to India he had been studying and living as a Buddhist monk in Columbo, then Ceylon and now Sri Lanka. You can see him for a split second in the film *The Bridge on the River Kwai* when a large group of monks in their yellow robes jump off the bridge. Grandad told me that actors were going to do this but then the monks decided to do it themselves in honour of their brothers who had died jumping off it in the war, under the Japanese. However, many of the Asian monks couldn't swim and the stipulation was that only swimmers would be allowed to participate, hence Grandad's five second starring role as a jumper. He loved the Buddhist way of life but he left the monastery after two years because trying to avoid stepping on every single ant became too much of a chore.

Grandad spent a couple of months with us in our flat in Hong Kong with his daughter Thelma, that is my mother, my father and us three little girls. He had lost his wife and younger daughter rather tragically, which had led to his leaving England in the first place. Now though, a few years later, he prowled restlessly around our apartment searching for the meaning of life.

It was therefore with a considerable sense of relief on all sides when he noticed an advertisement in the paper for a manager of the leper colony on the island of Hei Ling Chau.

Although leprosy was not an issue in Hong Kong itself, people had fled from China bringing the terrible disease with them. At the time they were cared for away from the general population, as was common in most countries.

Grandad leapt at the chance. In some ways he was well qualified for the job except that it was under the auspices of the English Methodist Church and his CV on the religious front was a little challenging. He had not only been a Buddhist and a Hindu but also an atheist, vegetarian Communist who had gone to Spain to fight the fascists, and a lecturer in Theosophy. Fortunately, Mum and Dad had joined the very respectable Union Church. The church had needed an organist and choirmaster, which Dad was very happy to take on, largely because he loved to play the organ, so Grandad was able to offer a pious family to the Methodists.

I wonder how many applicants they actually would have had anyway because I imagine in the 1950s people were very afraid of catching the disease. A treatment with sulphones was discovered and quickly discounted in the 1950s but it wasn't until 1981 that the World Health Organisation pronounced leprosy curable.

Apart from what might have been seen as his religious quirks, Grandad was eminently suitable. He was a master carpenter, though not for a time, as his last job in England had been as manager of the antiques department in Arding &

Hobbs in London. I remember him dressed in his tails as he had to be every day, allowing me as a little child to slide around on the highly polished surfaces of the grander items of furniture. He was also energetic, imaginative, well intentioned and single.

So off he went to Hei Ling Chau. It was about forty minutes from Hong Kong on a very small ferryboat. He was given a typical bungalow in the colonial style – teak furniture, wide verandahs, cool, green stone floors and a large garden overlooking the South China Sea, full of hibiscus and jasmine. We caught the little ferry to see him shortly after he moved and for a long time afterwards we went to visit Grandad on many weekends. The ferryboat had seating for six on each side and rolled and bucketed through the busy waterways until eventually reaching the tiny quay at Hei Ling Chau. The peace and the silence was immense after the bustle of Hong Kong.

Within a few weeks of his arrival Grandad was on his way to de-mystifying and re-integrating many of the lepers on the island. He managed to find a tractor somewhere and then found one of the residents to drive it. Somehow or other he also acquired a trailer with seating for six to attach to it. He either made himself, or got some of the residents to make, a jaunty red and white striped cover for the trailer complete with a fringe around the sides, to protect the passengers from sun or rain. This meant that those unable to walk far were suddenly able to travel around the island. Sitting in this we travelled slowly up the hill to Grandad's bungalow, along a red earth track surrounded by dense little pine trees.

He would have no truck, in general, with illness. This was after all the 1950s, when there was an atmosphere of possibilities and re-growth and people felt the world was heading towards a new dawn of modernity on many fronts. New discoveries were being made about the disease and new attitudes were coming into play. He overthrew the previous rule that non-leper family members couldn't live with their loved ones and gave them guidance about touching and other rudimentary precautions and suddenly there were a number of non-leperous people on the island, together with a sense of relief and happiness.

There had been an earlier plan to build a reservoir on Hei Ling Chau and Grandad was keen to see this through and so free the island from its dependence on the water boat. This became his passion and you can see the resultant dam briefly if you look up at the island when passing on the ferry from Hong Kong to Macau. It makes me proud to think of the difference he made to the lives of the inhabitants of Hei Ling Chau in so many ways.

Being a carpenter, he started designing

wooden parts for the afflicted lepers and teaching them how to make them, in a small workshop. New feet, for instance, were articulated in a simple way and could be strapped on to allow people to get around. Soon they were sporting new ears and noses all, where appropriate and possible, removable and easily fitted. My mother was dispatched to buy hats with false hair attached so that those with facial disfigurements and missing ears could feel more normal. People became encouraged, they grew their own food with help from their able-bodied families. Most of the patients had been agricultural workers and many were illiterate, which meant they had little to engage them, so they were very pleased to work on the land again.

Some were too ill to benefit from Grandad's exuberant plans. There was a good, caring but small hospital on the island, run by Dr Fraser and Matron, Miss Irene Moore. She was a lively, attractive middle-aged Canadian nurse, who had been in China since the age of nineteen and who spoke a number of Chinese dialects. She had been interned in Shanghai during the war and had also been at the Battle of Nanking. That will be a story for later on; suffice it to say she was a great friend of missionary Gladys Aylwood, the Small Woman of *The Inn of the Sixth Happiness*[7] fame, who was one of the fiercest and smallest women I have ever met.

Dr Fraser and his family, Miss Moore, and

Grandad lived about a quarter of a mile apart in their individual bungalows above the sea. We loved to visit Grandad there. Trudi and I would wander along a path away from the house through the dense pines until we reached a grove, which opened up into the sunshine, where butterflies in their hundreds fluttered everywhere in a cloud of blue. Unafraid, they would settle on Trudi's head, her arms and her hands, fly off and then come back again to cover her in a glittering blanket of blue and black. She has a way with animals. They rarely settled on me but they adored Trudi.

The background buzz of cicadas[8], the distant voices from Grandad's verandah, the occasional shout from our baby sister Sally and the particular smell of the ubiquitous pine trees, are things that I will never forget. Nor the freedom given to us to roam around the hillside with our plastic bottles of tepid orange squash hanging round our necks. We relished being in one of the healthiest places on the planet – if you didn't count the lepers who had, after all, caught leprosy in China before escaping.

One day Grandad called me to his side to tell me he had an important job for us. We were to put on our party dresses, which Mother had been instructed to bring, brush our hair and clean our teeth, and walk to Miss Moore's bungalow to deliver a special box of chocolates from Grandad, also brought under instruction by Mum. He told us in no uncertain terms to be charming, sweet, polite and gracious.

"As if we'd be anything else!" I complained darkly to my sister, I nine, she five-and-a-half, as we stomped off to Miss Moore's.

We presented her with the chocolates. There was a note attached. She laughed rather shrilly.

"Your grandad said could you wait just a minute, please?" she said, smiling and blushing. We waited. She read it. She blinked a few times, then she patted us on the heads.

"Tell him yes, and I'm on my way," she said. We walked back along the path through the pine trees. We had no idea what was going on.

"Miss Moore says 'yes' and she's on her way," I told Grandad. He picked me up and hugged me, a most unusual gesture from him but one he repeated fervently with Miss Moore a few minutes later, to our amazement.

And so it was that we acquired our new Granny, the delight of his life for Grandad and devoted to our family until she finally left us aged ninety-six, still the sweetest lady imaginable and with all her wits about her.

GRANNY

Having a new Granny in our family was a win-win for us. What a wonderful person, friend, support and fount of wisdom she was! I was nearly ten when she and my grandfather married, and my younger sister Trudi and I were bridesmaids. The ceremony took place at our church, the Union Church, an amalgamation of low Protestant churches where Dad was the organist and choirmaster, on a beautiful summer's day.

Although Grandad suffered a fall, which paralysed him from the waist down on the island of Hei Ling Chau several years later, their marriage was an extremely happy one. As Granny was such a practiced nurse, she coped better than anyone else could have done with the inevitable help that Grandad needed, with all her love and without a moment's hesitation.

Granny sang all the time. She was busy all the

time, too, and wore fearsome flip flops. As she hurried about with her characteristic slightly bent forward walk, her flip flops clicked against her heels in such a distinctive way you could hear her coming, flip flip flip, from all around the house.

She was a happy person, who had every reason not to have been happy at all. Aged nineteen Granny was left at the altar. The trauma of this can only be imagined. She came from a big farming family in Ontario. I think she was the second or third in a family of thirteen children. She had trained as a nurse rather than working on the family farm so her immediate decision, given that there was plenty of help for her parents was to leave the small town in Ontario where she lived, thereby avoiding seeing the man who had jilted her. She applied to the Canadian Mission Society as a nurse and took a ship to China.

Granny and Grandad

Granny was a diligent and hard working woman. She studied and learned the language. When we met almost thirty years later she spoke about five different Chinese dialects. It was quite frustrating, looking back, that I didn't ask her more about her extraordinary life when I had the chance. She was a great friend of the *Small Woman* Gladys Aylward, the heroine of the film later made of her life, entitled *The Inn of the Sixth Happiness* (see Appendix). Sometimes when Gladys visited Hong Kong she used to come and stay with us and terrify the life out of me. She was tiny and I towered above her when I was twelve or so and Granny and she were at our flat babysitting us.

Gladys was the fiercest woman I have ever met. She didn't approve of my lax upbringing one bit. I'm not surprised, she had marched umpteen children to safety over the mountains of China to escape the murderous Japanese, which must have meant strict order and obedience on their part, so she was less than impressed with me wanting to stay up past my bedtime.

Gladys Aylward[9] was perhaps the best Christian ever to hit China. A short resume of her life is included in the Appendix. She actually adopted an unknown number of Chinese orphans, too. I suppose I should mention, for those who have seen the film *The Inn of the Sixth Happiness*, which is the romanticised story of her trek with the children, she absolutely and categorically denied ever having any love affair with any Japanese army officer. She had only once been in love and that was with a Chinese Colonel but their marriage plans sadly ended up coming to nothing.

It is astonishing what events Granny and other missionaries lived through in China at the time. The worst she told me about was the Siege of Nanking by the Japanese in early June 1937. There were a number of foreigners living in Nanking at the time, as it was the capital city of Eastern China and Granny was one of them. She was working as a senior nurse. She wasn't involved in missionary work but I believe her diligence, devotion and practicality was the best advertisement for the simplest Christian message of all – love thy neighbour as thyself.

The situation in brief was that the Japanese had annexed three areas of Eastern China and called them Manchuria. There was no love lost between China and Japan historically – the story in China, which of course influenced me considerably, having friends whose parents had been interned by the Japanese army at Stanley prison in Hong Kong and treated abysmally, was that a certain Emperor of China's daughter had been walking in the walled garden of the palace when an ape had climbed the wall and raped her. Her father, who loved her and didn't want to kill her after this incident, took her to an island and left her there, alive, where she had the resultant baby. Thus the Japanese race began.

The Japanese in Manchuria began to expand into the rest of Eastern China, and as they did so attacked and besieged Nanking in 1937. Why they were so utterly brutal is something still discussed in academia. The best explanation I have read lists several contributory reasons:

The general Japanese hatred (resentment? Jealousy?) of the Chinese

the troops tired and on starvation

rations

the directive from the Emperor to terrify
the Chinese to dishearten them

errant and improperly trained leaders

untrained troops mainly made up of
reservists

anger in general not curtailed by any
cohesive military restraints.

The list goes on. I think it boils down to hungry,
angry men given licence to kill, maim and rape
an enemy's women and children with no holds
barred.

Granny was Christian but as she said,
sometimes humanity has to come before
everything. Information about the Japanese
troops' behaviour as they advanced on Nanking
spread in advance of their arrival and alerted
the young women to their cruelty. The troops
used the babies for bayonet practice, throwing
them into the air and catching them with their
bayonets. The idea was, apparently, to spear
them on the arm or leg so as not to kill them
but to be able to use them alive several times.
When they had finished with the babies they
gang raped the broken women, using themselves
and any other instruments to hand, including

the bayonets.

The young women fled out of the city to the city walls. They hugged and kissed their babies, and then, after a few minutes, swung them by their legs and bashed their heads against the walls as hard as they could, killing them instantly. The girls screamed as they did this, Granny told me, and then they killed themselves with kitchen knives, either into their hearts or slitting their throats. If they couldn't, their friends helped.

"But Granny," I said – I was about fifteen when she told me this in a matter-of-fact way - "surely as Christians we should never kill?"

"They were already as good as dead. It's just the time and the method that changed," she said. Granny did not help to kill them but she helped them to go to the wall and she helped them keep their strength.

Her friend Gladys took about a hundred children and marched with them into and through the mountains to escape; she must have needed them to obey her instantly and to believe in her completely and she saved their lives. The Japanese put a price on all their heads to try and stop them escaping. Gladys herself was particularly wanted by the Japanese and they put a bounty of $100 - a fortune, on her head - that is if anyone had dared to capture her.

Granny was interned by the Japanese in Shanghai in the British Embassy, the author

JG Ballard[10] was held there, too. In fact, the English speaking Lieutenant in charge of the internees wanted to make amends in some way for Nanking. He constantly asked them how he could make their lives better. For instance, Granny asked him to find a piano tuner so they could have some entertainment if he could, and he did. This made their imprisonment a little easier, as they could then play the piano and sing. They had enough to eat and were not harmed. I mention this to balance all the other dreadful things the Japanese did.

Granny wrote copious records of events during her entire time in China, and I have donated them all to the University of Hong Kong for their reference library. The sad thing, as far as I am concerned though, is that she burnt all the references to her love affair with Grandad, which of course was what I wanted to read! I remonstrated with her – she was ninety by then and Grandad long dead – and her reply was just, "All that's private, Mary! I don't want anyone reading that!"

Hmm. Little did she know everyone would have liked the personal stories rather than just the historical information. Or maybe she did.

Here is the poem my Canadian Granny wrote in 1941. Eighty-three years ago and what has changed?

TO A ROAD

Before the feet of armies trod this way
oh road of China, you were old and wise,
whom do you see, throughout the dreary
days?
What hear, as seasons fall and rise?

There is the constant thud of passing feet
and burdened hearts sunk deep in
misery,
with tragedy and pain in every beat
they know, in war, their souls;
Gethsemane.

But what, oh road, of those who stand on
guard?
As straight as shining bayonet; longside,
the conquering horde whose hand is firm
and hard
who ever strive to hold aloft their pride.

They stand so close beside me, in a trice -
when thoughts of home come surging
over them
their souls gaze through - at last -
unguarded eyes
and thoughts flood in, impossible to
stem.

One stoops in pity at the pain of some
whose disillusioned lips are curled in

scorn,

but sadder far, it seems, are those who come

bewildered, young, from country hillsides torn.

For centuries when armies inroads made
with dreams of conquest and the lust for power
invader and invaded likewise paid
for such was war; and still so at this hour.

But yonder are the rice fields, fresh and green

give hope and courage in our troubled state.

When gallant Morning Glories ruin screen -

then truth and love shall overshadow hate.

Irene Hanford, *nee Moore*
Canton, October 1941

SUNSET PEAK

Sunset Peak

"No, I most certainly will not!" declared my Grandmother.

"But Mother..."

"I said no, Harold!"

Dad looked unhappy. Nana stood firm. The coolie porters, their tanned legs knotted with muscle and their faces seamed and brown from the sun watched with interest, their smiles revealing the one or two teeth left in their mouths.

We were standing beside a sandy track at the base of Hong Kong's tallest mountain, Lantau

Peak$_{11}$ on Lantau Island. It loomed above us, its tip lost in the clouds. Behind the coolies a rocky path rose upwards. The driver of the van which had delivered us here, cheerfully unloaded our holiday bags, dumped them at the side of the track, waved and roared off in a cloud of dust.

Two coolies lashed our bags onto their bamboo poles with thin strips of bamboo. The other two stood watching with interest, smoking the stinking little brown cigarettes that seemed to fortify them. I watched as well, guiltily, because I'd been told not to bring more than three books due to weight and actually my bag was full of them - at over ten I constantly had my nose in a book. The coolies adjusted the wads of padding on their shoulders, slung their yokes across them and set off up the mountain. Our stuff was gone. Now we just had to get Nana up there, too.

Luckily we only had to walk up to the top of the second tallest mountain, Sunset Peak. There, above the cloud line, was a collection of stone huts once used by the army and now transformed into a Christian missionary holiday camp. Our Canadian step-Granny who had connections as she had been a missionary nurse, had kindly arranged this holiday for us to get away from Hong Kong island's exhausting summer heat.

As it took most of the day to climb the mountain, Dad considered it too much for his mother so he was determined to get her into the sedan chair he'd hired to carry her up to the camp. The porters watched curiously while Dad implored her to get into the battered, wooden sedan chair to be conveyed precariously up the steep path upon their shoulders, something she categorically did not want to do.

Eventually, tight-lipped and terrified, she gave up and he helped her climb into it and sit on the stained red satin cushions.

"I won't go in the horrible chair!" cried my little sister, recoiling.

"No, darling," said Mother soothingly, "only Nana's going in the horrible chair, we're going on a lovely walk! And Daddy'll carry you when you get tired," whereupon Dad gave her a dark look. We watched as the sedan chair was lifted off the ground. The grimy curtains swung apart and we saw Nana's panicked face as her arthritic fingers clutched its peeling ochre paint. The coolies settled Nana onto their shoulders and the sedan chair rocked and swayed as they set off briskly up the mountain. The porters moved in perfect synchronicity, the wooden poles bouncing off their shoulders as they went. The first part of the journey was so steep they had to go sideways. Poor Nana!

With our water bottles around our necks, peanut butter sandwiches, grapes and apples in our backpacks, we started up the path. After an hour or so we arrived at a grassy meadow, where we stopped for a snack and did a few cartwheels with Mum, then continued up the path, winding around the hillside, sometimes very steeply, until another level glade appeared. The smell of pine trees enveloped us, and cicadas buzzed us on our way, until finally we rose above the cloud line and reached the damp and misty top. Out of the clouds loomed the first camp building.

The holidaymakers at the camp were clean and hearty Americans, fervent in their love of Jesus. Although we too loved Jesus, we didn't normally say, "Praise Jesus!" in every sentence, like they did. Two very clean teenage boys led us to our cabin, which was more like a hut, up a wet and slippery stepping-stone path. We could only see about two feet in front of us because the mist was dense and it was getting darker by the minute.

"Don't fall in the pool!" laughed one of the holy pair. We looked sideways. Beside the lethal path there was a large, murky natural pool inches from our feet with dark green, impenetrable water. A cacophony of frogs started honking. I hurried past; nobody was going to force me to swim in that. I was grateful I'd disobeyed and brought a pile of books with me.

Our hut was a two room affair, with bunks and a child's bed in the back room and more bunks in the front and an arch between them. There was a wash basin you filled with a bucket from an outdoor tap but we had to use the communal toilet block at the main building, which was also where we had our meals and praised Jesus. We roamed around, only discovering some damp *Reader's Digests* and jigsaw puzzles on a shelf.

But where was Nana? We asked ourselves urgently. We rushed out to catch up with the descending boys, demanding our grandmother. Don't worry, they said, she'd been delivered to her room in the main building, which was equipped with a real bed, and was cheerful since her ordeal had not catapulted her into a mountainous cleft, nor had she been bitten by a cobra and left to die. In fact once she stopped aching she seemed delighted with her adventure, a source of much interest on her return to Broadstairs, Kent.

Supper was at six, so we wiped our sweaty faces and gingerly negotiated the slippery stepping-stone path back to the main building. The clouds parted intermittently and the wet black stones reflected the starlight as we slid along in our inadequate flip flops. When we entered the dining room, we found two rows of wooden tables and chairs filled with beaming soldiers of the Lord. We were introduced warmly by the woman in charge, then sat down to sing grace. "Thank you for the world so sweet, thank you for the food we eat, thank you for the birds that sing, thank you God for everything," we all sang at the tops of our voices. I've never again been in such relentlessly cheerful company.

The food was unlike anything we'd ever had; macaroni cheese from tins, Angel Delight, rice with tinned peas and carrots, something called tuna bake comprising tinned tuna, tinned soup and tinned corn with tinned macaroni cheese on top, baked. Most food had Campbell's chicken or mushroom soup in it. There was orange Tang, which you mixed with water, but was delicious fizzing on your tongue in powder form.

Mother assumed we would all get scurvy. Within minutes she was desperately asking for some fresh vegetables, which didn't seem to feature with God's American children, but she was horrified to discover there wouldn't be anyone portering up for a week. She spent the week berating herself for not staggering up the mountain burdened with pounds of healthy vegetables for her beloved family but we didn't care, we were happy enough with plain rice, of which there was always plenty.

Some days dawned wonderfully clear and sunny, the views were stupendous, the air clean, the feeling of joy deep, the ball games and walks and handstand practice and whatever else we did, magical. Nana was bolstered by knowing she would be allowed to walk back down the mountain on her own two feet and she and I sat in the sun and played Test Your Word Power from the limp pages of the *Reader's Digests*.

Other days it rained and the cloud cover was dense. We slid our way to the main building in our transparent plastic macs for a breakfast of cereal and powdered milk. Afterwards we went back to our hut, where I demanded my reading time against everybody else's wishes. Dad wanted me to play battleships and Mum pretended to think I'd enjoy helping my sisters to do jigsaw puzzles.

But I ignored them all and lay on my bunk on the thin, plastic-covered mattress in a humid pool of sweat, my fingers sticking to the damp pages of authors like Ray Bradbury and Arthur C Clarke telling tales of alien civilizations. Trickles of sweat stung as they dripped into my eyes and rolled down my neck into my hair, and I breathed deeply the unforgettable smell of sweaty plastic, mould and Mother's daily wiping down with diluted Dettol.

All too soon we packed our sodden effects into our bags to be carried back down the mountain, ambled down ourselves with our victorious Grandmother, and took the ferry home to Hong Kong.

Now the Missionary holiday homes are gone, their stones fallen into the grass, the mountain has reclaimed them. Few people now alive ever went there, most are gone - my grandmothers are long dead, my parents, too. Another time, another age, another wonderful life.

FIRST LEAVE

After a few months had passed our parents decided to extend Father's contract and commit to a long-term stay in Hong Kong. We lived in a beautiful, big flat on the Peak, adopted a dog called Penny, had bought the car of Dad's dreams and I had settled at school. The icing on the cake was that he was employed long-term on the old, colonial contract set up when Hong Kong was a malarial, disease-ridden nightmare, reasonably considered a hardship posting. Well, it had been once! Two years later the contract was changed to a six week holiday by air, but we still had six months by ship first class for all of us, or the financial equivalent. It's obvious what Dad chose to do! And Mother had decided that having an amah was actually quite surprisingly helpful. On top of that my asthma was so much better it was almost forgotten.

But what was not forgotten was the sorrowful sight of Dad's mother, Nana, standing alone at Southampton dock as we sailed away. So, Nana joined us a little later for a protracted stay. She settled into her own bedroom and bathroom and it was lovely having her around because she was such a cheerful, stable lady happy to join in with everything we did in spite of what I thought of at the time was her age – she was actually under seventy and very fit. How time changes perspective!

Nana had shared all the new experiences we

had with us, the different foods, the alarming trip up to Sunset Peak, but perhaps what she liked most was to take little Sally for walks in her pushchair around Harlech Road to the waterfall. I can picture them now in my mind's eye, Sally with her *helmet* haircut and Nana in one of her many floral dresses, standing by the railings hand in hand watching the water coming over the rocks. Years later, I, too, took my little son to stand there and watch the same waterfall when he was the same age. In between, as teenagers we regularly climbed the vertical waterfall - *Forbidden to Climb* ordered the metal sign – we used the sign as a hand hold - and idled hours away in the stream above it.

Eventually the time came for us all to return to England for our first six month's *leave*. Thus began the prototype for Dad's convoluted and action-packed long trips. This time he chose to take us, for a treat, on a popular posh ship called the Victoria. It was owned by Lloyd Triestino$_{12}$, a swanky Italian shipping line noted for its glamour, panache and fancy food. We all travelled first class and very nice it was too; a pianist in white tails played the grand piano every evening, there were concerts with opera singers, the food was wonderful and the whole elegantly continental atmosphere differed somewhat from P&O.

All went well. We children were, by now, very familiar with spaghetti. We cruised gently from Hong Kong stopping here and there until we arrived in Karachi, Pakistan. We moored in the bay and were delivered to shore by smart launches, where we explored a little but quickly returned with relief to the cool sophistication of our ship. It was extremely hot, so the air conditioning on board was really welcome.

We were due to stay in Karachi for just a couple of days. Then disaster struck! There was a total seaman's strike called in Italy. Every member of the crew went on strike. They closed and locked the saloon and bar. Everywhere but our cabins was locked up. They would not operate anything on the ship including the kitchen and the air conditioning. Everything simply stopped.

Then the irritated and inconvenienced Karachi Port Authorities in their turn refused to allow the ship to remain moored in the harbour and moved us to the very end of an extremely long, unused oil wharf. It was boiling hot, more so because out of the bay there was no longer a sea breeze. I will never forget the vision of the wharf's bitumen surface melting and shimmering in the sun.

After 24 hours or so it became obvious the strike was not going to be resolved easily or soon. Quickly some of the Ambassadors of the various countries with passengers on board started to organise evacuations. Needless to say, the Americans went first; collected in limousines and taken off to the airport to be flown home.

Meanwhile, the exasperated British Ambassador was obliged to return from his holiday in the mountains to do something about us. He arranged not for our evacuation, but for us to be collected by gharry, a battered old horse-drawn carriage, and taken to the Metropole Hotel in Karachi during the day, where we were given dry chicken sandwiches of sliced white bread curling in the heat and bottles of pop. The gharries couldn't be driven to us at the ship because the road was too sticky for the horses' hooves, so we had to walk what seemed a mile to get to them, our shoes sticking to the melting tarmac with every step.

Very soon after the Americans, the Canadians were spirited away. They felt rather bad about leaving what was becoming a close-knit little band of warriors, who spent a lot of time trying to shame the crew into opening the food stores and allowing us to have tins of things. Absolutely not. They would not hear of it. Then the Italians passengers left, and the French.

There we were, being carted off to the dilapidated hotel every day, eating our truly awful sandwiches at rusting iron tables on the straggly dry grass. Mother would not allow us to eat any salad or fruit other than bananas, the skins of which she wiped with antiseptic before we peeled them. Returning to the ship in the late afternoon, we were greeted by the sight of the crew in their vests and boxer shorts lined up at the railings, fishing and drinking beer.

By this time there were some Scandinavians, Dutch, one or two Australians and a few others as well as our family remaining but we were a much reduced group of leftovers, whose Ambassadors seemed unwilling to rescue. Finally, Nana cracked. Under her supervision the men managed to get the locked saloon door open. Then hands on hips she said firmly, "Harold, you should break the locks on the bar. Then we can all have a drink."

Several gentlemen rushed to obey. The bar, made of ornate and highly polished wood, was locked and shuttered. Somebody got a crowbar or something similar and broke the lock. The shutters were pulled open and the shelves inside, with their sparkling glasses and full bottles were revealed in all their glory.

"Now, let's get this piano unlocked, too!" cried Nana.

"Right-O Mother," said Dad and the several gentlemen cheerfully levered open the extremely expensive piano with a little splintering of the wooden lid.

The elusive captain, never normally seen or heard from when anyone tried to remonstrate with him, appeared from somewhere.

"Hey!" he cried, or the equivalent in Italian, "You cannot do that! Leave the bar and the piano alone! It must be locked! This room is not open for passengers!"

Chance would be a fine thing. Somebody was already behind the bar pouring drinks, and we watched wide-eyed as the captain was told in no uncertain terms what he could do and where he could go, while being bundled bodily out of the room and the door bolted behind him.

In a matter of moments Father was at the piano, and in a spirit of high hilarity everyone started singing. We were of course locked in, or rather the captain and crew were locked out, but there were plenty of crisps, olives, nuts and little cheesy cocktail biscuits – a veritable feast - behind the bar, and lots of juice for us children.

One by one, the other nationalities were rescued, until there was only us. Literally. We six were the only British passengers and the only ones left behind. Dad got gastroenteritis and to his credit the ship's doctor and the nurse came from the ship's medical centre to give him medicines and an intravenous drip as he had lost so much fluid. I also had a bout of it so I was lying in the other bed while Mother flitted between us. Apparently, it was touch and go for Dad. I am very glad I hadn't realised that at the time. Actually, I think I knew it was extremely serious, but what do you really understand at nearly eleven?

The British Ambassador finally seemed shamed into doing something about us - presumably he had been alerted to the fact that the possible demise of a British passenger would not do a lot for his career prospects. Shortly afterwards we were collected by car, with our luggage, and taken to the airport to be transported on probably the most wonderful plane I have ever been on - SAS, the Swedish airline. There were only six seats in first class so we were alone and they were superb, wide, cool leather chairs that reclined almost flat. We lay back. We six had two stewardesses who seemed to be very sorry for us and plied us with sumptuous food. We were in heaven.

And so we flew in great style to our next stop, Geneva, where Nana left us and flew home. We went by train to Kandersteg, Switzerland, to frolic in the daisies on the mountains, discover the wonders of duvets, climb up with a plastic bag to collect snow to show Sally, and eat an awful lot of hearty vegetable soup. Mother was thrilled and sang all day.

FUN WITH ANIMALS

Fun and animals: Sally with Penny, Mum with Wendy

Everyone in our family loved animals, so consequently we had a broad-ranging selection during our life in Hong Kong. Once we'd settled into our flat on the Peak, we had headed off to the HKSPCA and found ourselves a dog. She was a typical motley cocktail of chow-chow, a bit of terrier and a bit of Alsatian, with a black nose and eyes and furthermore a black spotty tongue as so many Hong Kong dogs do. Her fur was glossy and thick and the colour of maple syrup. She was a good dog and we loved her, particularly when she had four sweet balls of fluffy puppies, so we were very sad when we later discovered she had cancer. In fact, prior to the puppies' arrival I inadvertently witnessed her and a little boy dog *in flagrante delicto* in the car park when she had been let out for five minutes for a wee, which was rather difficult for Dad to explain to me at eight – I kept calling her to me and telling Dad she was unhappily stuck. The poor little boy dog was being dragged across the car park by her trying to come to me. I have no idea what Dad said to me about this as I was so young. Probably not a lot! Life presents you with these imponderables.

Having lost poor Penny to cancer, we returned to England on our first leave, whereupon Mother decided we should get an English dog with credentials and not risk another rescue one which could be ill and leave us prematurely. She had a fancy for a poodle. Off we went to the posh poodle breeder somewhere in the heart of Surrey and there we found our long-term dog, who was with us for our whole childhood. She was sixteen years old when she eventually left us. I remember sitting in the car with the new puppy on Mum's lap while we thought of names for her. Unfortunately (and it could have been me), one of us came up with Wendy. So Wendy she was.

Wendy was a miniature white poodle with a massive personality. She came everywhere with us, swimming, climbing, walking, boating... you name it. She was tough. And she was fixated on Mum. As she grew older she became ever more peculiar and there were two things I particularly think about at that stage.

We always had cats - and more about that later. During her early and middle years Wendy tolerated them moderately well, but her behaviour towards them as an old lady was 'very naughty', as Mother used to say indulgently. In the late afternoon Wendy would lurk behind a particular chair, watching the cats silently. There was a large area of polished parquet flooring between her lurking chair and the chairs and sofas on the other side of the room, which were suitable landing places for cats.

The cats prowled along the cushions on the backs of the sofas by the verandah, building up courage to scamper across the floor in full sight of the dog and make their way, by using these various safe, though distant, chairs and sofas, to get to their dinner. Eventually of course they'd have to chance it and there would be a flurry of cat claws sliding about on the polished floor as Wendy launched herself at them from her hiding place – with eyes wide, fur bristling and squeals of outrage from the cats. Wendy would bark and skid across the floor until the cats could leap up on to something, growling and complaining in high dudgeon.

"That was very naughty, Wendy," Mum would remark gently from behind her newspaper. Meanwhile we all shouted, "Wendy! No!"

"She doesn't mean any harm," said Mum. Looking at the dog's wild eyes and her tongue hanging out of her mouth, we weren't so sure.

Wendy's main other naughtiness was to do with her being peeved with Mum if she stayed out later than Wendy deemed acceptable. She would walk very deliberately into their bedroom, jump on the bed, dig around on Mum's pillow and then christen the centre of it with a little wee. There's not a lot less pleasant than climbing into bed tired after a night out and snuggling down into a pillow wet with doggy wee. Poor Mum. It makes me laugh now to think of her at two o'clock in the morning roaming around with a sodden pillow and saying, "That's very naughty, Wendy."

Mother thought she and Wendy could make their fortunes with pure-bred Kennel Registered puppies. There were a few issues militating against this, however. Wendy only had four puppies and that was after three meetings with her partner whose services were costly and, frankly, very much unwanted by Wendy.

Mum decided to keep one puppy who she named Tammy. After all the injections, the special food, the time, the registrations, the fact that two of them were boys and so less valuable and so on, the scheme was not after all a stupendous financial success. Wendy (and possibly Mum) got somewhat fed up with pandering to the puppies after they were about ten weeks old – potential homes had to be inspected and all in all, I think Mum and Wendy just about broke even. All the puppies of course were found wonderful homes so it wasn't a disaster. Wendy, however, was not thrilled to have Tammy in her life – or should I say, Mum's life - and in the end a great friend of Mother's took her on and life returned to normal.

We children were always finding kittens. The feral cats weren't spayed and lived harrowing lives outside, fending for themselves unless a use could be found by someone for them as ratters. We found them shoved into cracks in walls, in the streets, in the bushes, in plastic bags – everywhere you looked there were scrawny, sick little miaowing kittens and of course we wanted to save them all. We did save quite a few of them. We usually had about two or three cats, but when we came home with a fourth, our parents said that was it. We had to take them to the HKSPCA where they were euthanised by the dozen. I realised when I was quite young that this was inevitable and they didn't cry, they nestled together in a box, the lid was closed, a quick acting gas was released and they went to sleep. I made myself watch this once. It has made me very pragmatic; pain I won't tolerate but I am realistic about how many kittens can be saved and cared for properly.

My own cat was called Princess Pru. She was a very pretty little white cat who I carried around when I was ten or eleven, and whispered all my secrets to. None of us realised, until Mum read about white cats frequently being deaf, that she wasn't just a typically superior cat when she didn't come when called or pay any attention to anyone unless you picked her up – she was, in fact, as deaf as a post. I didn't care, I loved her.

One evening Mother, Father and I went to see a production at the junior school starring Trudi, and when we returned home we found Princess Pru dead on the side of the road. Stark beneath the street light black blood scarred her white fur. She must have followed us without our noticing. I was heartbroken; it was my first experience of the death of a loved one. Dad picked her up and we brought her home. Mum wrapped her in a towel so I could hold her to say goodbye, and then Dad took her away.

At our flat Father decided to build a walk-in aviary. It all started when we were given a pair of budgies in a cage but Dad felt this was not good enough for the birds. He built a frame over one third of our very large open balcony and covered it with fine mesh, with a door so we could go in and talk to them. Thus he proceeded to create a budgie paradise. He dragged trees up the stairs to put in it, together with swings, perching ledges, hoops, bells, ladders and all sorts of budgie entertainment – although from what I can remember they mostly sat in a row on the barren topmost tree branch no matter how seductive Dad's innovations were.

Soon the budgies laid eggs. Dad had provided all manner of nests but they actually just laid them on the floor; they're an unpretentious type of bird. So there were the eggs on the floor and we all chose one which Dad marked with our initials. They all hatched. Imagine our excitement – our own birds! I was thrilled. My budgie grew and thrived. She was a lovely colour, pale pink and grey and I called her Pearl.

Pearl turned out to be the Empress of Russia of budgies. She was the ultimate stroppy bird and would bite you as soon as she looked at you – but she was beautiful! Dad even suggested we find another home for her when we stood together looking at Pearl, sitting in glorious isolation on a branch while the hapless others huddled together at the far end of the aviary. But no, I wouldn't have it, and Pearl ruled the roost for a number of years into the future.

At the other end of this same balcony we had our guinea pig cage. They were sweet animals and we enjoyed playing with them. I so loved their little gurgling, squeaking noises – the amazing sight of tiny newborn guinea pigs looking like identical clones of great big ones was spell binding! We soon learned though, if new baby guinea pigs had been born we had to keep away from them for at least a week, because otherwise the mother would eat them. Oh how revolted we were! Life for animals seemed so dreadful. Mother created a hideaway for the guinea pigs with bamboo mats and we stayed away with trepidation, hoping there would still be some babies when we eventually could look at them and play with them again.

Mother could cope with guinea pigs. Mice however, were not on her acceptable pet list. Sadly for her, when I was in the final year at our junior school, Peak School, mice as fashion accessories were all the rage. We children all had tiny brown and white mice running, climbing and spinning in their cages on all their equipment and we brought them to school, too. We put them down the fronts of our school uniform dresses and let them run around. We would stroke them and play with them when they eventually scampered down our arms and arrived, as they inevitably did, into our hands.

Mother was not happy with this mouse addiction of ours, to say the least, and neither was Ah Chun. I had to take my mouse house outside onto the back staircase because of the mousey smell, alleged by Mother to be overpowering but as far as I was concerned, undetectable. It was my duty to change and clean their home; Mother would have nothing to do with them. They made her shudder, she said. They were very sweet I seem to remember. I have no idea what happened to them but I assume Mother prevailed and the mice returned from whence they had come.

Some time after the mouse scenario my little sister developed a penchant for baby terrapins. They took over my sisters' bath in which my sisters had created a terrapin heaven. There were flat rocks and rounded rocks, bridges, plastic fish and whales, arches made of plaster and painted like antique Chinese heirlooms, old Chinese plaster men with fishing rods and various Gods and Goddesses, too. The little terrapins lumbered about in bewilderment amongst all this sumptuous bath furniture while we watched them, sitting on the edge of the bath. Looking back, it was a shame to have these little turtles but at the time all the children were into terrapinalia and so I can't criticise anyone now.

Needless to say, there were a number of other creatures enjoying the hospitality of our flat – some less welcome than others - so every three months the Government Pest Control operatives descended upon us, much to the chagrin of

Mother and the suspicions of Ah Chun. They were an intimidating bunch, arriving absolutely to the minute of the appointed time. There were four coolies in bright blue overalls and masks, controlled and directed by the magnificent Chief Infestation and Rodent Control Officer. He was dressed very like a senior police officer in a smart, deep navy blue uniform, crisp white shirt and a fancy white officer's hat. He looked round with a supercilious expression, before barking instructions to the frightened coolies with their various death-dealing puffers and sprays, who obediently crawled around the floor and poked their weapons into every nook and cranny. At the end of all this, the Chief Infestation Officer evaluated the work of the coolies while they crouched silently on the floor, then gave Mother a chitty to sign with a nifty little bow, and off they went in military fashion. I wasn't aware of dead rats or cockroaches or in fact anything untoward, but I suppose it must have been effective because I don't remember too much infestation either.

However, Ah Chun was always delighted when a big fat cockroach flew in through the window and ran across the floor of the kitchen. She'd quickly shake off her black slipper and catch it with her bare foot, then drop it into a small bottle of oil and put it on the window sill. There were a number of them in varying stages of decay lined up in front of the kitchen window. Eventually the insect would disappear completely, dissolved into the increasingly disgusting, yellowing oil, whereupon the oil would acquire magical properties – excellent for bruises, aches and pains, sore heads and other things I don't remember. I was not keen to have cockroach oil rubbed into me and absolutely refused to let her do it, to the consternation of my dear amah who only wanted to ease my random suffering.

One day, when I was almost adult, Sally joined her friends to go off to Cheung Chau island for a day out and when she returned she wasn't alone. She'd found a little brown puppy, an absolute bundle of joy, pretty, appealing, lost and alone. Hey ho. Little did we know how that was going to turn out! She named the sweet, tiny thing Pud, short for Pudding. I suppose he did look a bit soft and round and puddingy at that stage. He was very like our long lost Penny; a typical Hong Kong mixture. And he was adorable then.

However, our time in Hong Kong was coming to a close. As per his contract, Father was required to retire at fifty-five years old. This was for two reasons, firstly because at the time his old-fashioned contract was first issued, Hong Kong was considered a hardship posting (quite a stretch of the imagination now) and therefore it was assumed employees would be desperate to go home to the green, cold country of their birth. Secondly, they needed to get rid of the upper echelons so that the younger people coming up behind them could have their turn at the top.

Mother was quite happy to leave. Everything was packed up. They had bought a house in Cornwall. I was married and living in Moscow, Trudi was living in Cape Town, and Sally was due to finish her A-levels, which she did in Cornwall. By that time Mum and Dad hadn't any more cats and only had Trudi's dog Tarka and Sally's dog, the now fully grown and infamous Pud, to transport back to England.

I suppose, as our parents somewhat bitterly said, it was rather an expensive burden they had taken upon themselves on behalf of two of their daughters, since both dogs cost a fortune to fly over and then be quarantined for six months. Well, what are parents for? We ask ourselves.

Pud was born a Hong Kong pack dog from the islands. He erupted into the peace and tranquillity of the Cornish countryside like a firecracker, all guns blazing. He couldn't believe his luck – fields, sheep, space! Trying to control Pud, raging with passion and testosterone, was like trying to control the wind, but Dad did try very hard and Sally's boyfriend, who was latterly her husband, did as well. But try as they might Pud did very occasionally manage to do the odd runner and soon every clutch of puppies for miles around looked strangely brown, with thick, glossy fur the colour of maple syrup, long lost echoes of Penny. Many a sheepdog bears a trace of Pud's colouring even now, but as a dog he was totally unaggressive so all was not lost by his speedy, if unwanted, integration into the Cornish canine fold.

And my brother-in-law taught him a lesson regarding sheep that he never forgot - that would have been a whole different story. Pud steered well clear of sheep for the rest of his life.

AUNTIE MARY

We were returning to Hong Kong from our first leave, but after our experiences on the glamorous Italian passenger ship Victoria, our parents decided to travel at completely the opposite end of the scale, on a small cargo ship belonging to the Blue Funnel line. It was called the Perseus and carried around thirty passengers at the time. It was comfortable and the food was excellent, being staffed by an Indian crew.

Being a cargo ship we had to make a number of stops at commercial quays, including Holland in the middle of winter. It was freezing cold on the docks at the port of Rotterdam in early January 1958, but we didn't feel it as we ran along the huge tree trunks, which had been off-loaded into a pile on the dock-side. They had been shipped in from the virgin rainforests of the Dutch East Indies, now known as Indonesia. I feel quite differently about them now, over six decades later, than I did then, when I saw them only as a mighty wooden mountain for us to leap about on. We ran along them through the fine snow that drifted around us, and leapt from one to the other to see how far we could jump.

I was with another girl called Amanda who

was also going back to Hong Kong on the Dutch cargo ship, and we were supposed to be doing our homework. She called herself Billy and had very short hair. We got along well even though she wanted to be a boy and refused to wear dresses like me – de rigour in those days – and if her parents insisted on a skirt she'd only wear a kilt.

So there we were in the slippery snow running along these massive, heavy logs, when suddenly a ferocious voice barked, "What do you think you're doing?"

We both stopped in our tracks and turned to look at whoever it was. There stood an imposing Englishman, upright as a ramrod, and frowning at us angrily. Beside him stood a glamorous black-haired lady wrapped in furs.

"Get down from there at once!" he shouted. We stared at him. Who was he? But we scuttled down anyway.

"Those logs could roll down at any minute and crush you! You stupid, stupid children!"

"Sorry," we muttered.

"Get back on board! I'll have to speak to your fathers."

We climbed up the gangplank onto the ship and I was just about to slink away when the lady took my hand.

"Don't worry about him, he was just frightened for you. I'll talk to your mummy," she whispered in an exotic accent. And she did and the whole affair was forgotten, except that

Auntie Mary and Uncle Ralty had come into our lives, never to leave them again until the day they died in their late nineties.

They had met in Shanghai. Uncle Ralty was a young lieutenant in the Royal Navy, only nineteen years old. He was on his first mission to China and had just arrived in Shanghai when he joined several other young men to go to the exciting Shanghai Bund for a break from the ship. At the time there were many young women in Shanghai of various nationalities, who had ended up on the edge of China and who were keen to go out, drink cocktails, go dancing and have a good time. Auntie Mary was one of them.

She herself was partly Portuguese from Macau. I think her grandfather contributed this bit; she was therefore partly Chinese as well since Macanese people are both and she was strictly Catholic. She was also, like so many others, partly white Russian. White Russians had fled all the way across Russia into China then, via Hunan. They had worked their way down through China until landing in Shanghai. Many moved on to Hong Kong too. In the 1950s it was common to see gangs of white Russians working on the roads in Kowloon. Shanghai, being such a large trading port, had room for all sorts of businessmen of all nationalities, including English, Scottish and Chinese of course. It was lively, exciting, dynamic and also no doubt a little decadent.

Auntie Mary described her life in Shanghai to me over the years. It sounded staggeringly wonderful to me when I was in my teens! She had left the convent where she had been educated when she was eighteen. She lived in her own private rooms with a family, not hers directly I believe, and she revelled in a life of luxury. Her amah woke her at about eleven o'clock in the morning with a cup of chocolate and any mail, then she soaked in a perfumed bath. At about noon she went by sedan chair or rickshaw to have lunch, either with friends or with some young man who considered himself fortunate beyond words to be allowed to pay for her Champagne. Then there was shopping, or mahjong, followed by tea. Home again to sleep until it was time for the cocktail parties to begin – and of course dinner. But the best part was yet to come. After dinner there was dancing until the early hours of the morning. She would come home at three or four and go to bed, not to be disturbed until eleven the following morning. Flirtation, yes. Sex, no.

One day she met Ralty, a shy Englishman two years younger than herself. At first she enjoyed flirting and teasing him but though they seemed an unlikely match they fell head over heels in love. He returned to England to his upperclass home, declared his love for Mary and asked his father for permission to marry her. His father apparently went berserk, "A little foreign good-time girl you met at the docks?!" I believe he said, or words to that effect, and when Ralty, enraged, refused to back down, his father disinherited him. This was quite a big deal. He lost everything.

Ralty returned to Shanghai under some stress, for now there was trouble in China and foreigners were no longer welcome. Japan had invaded and created Manchuria, Shanghai lost much of its status and power and war was declared. But Mary had no citizenship, so Ralty hired a small riverboat to smuggle her down the Pearl River, hiding under the deck beneath a load of sacking. They travelled at night with the (well-bribed) boatmen hiding her and it was very dangerous as there were both soldiers and bandits lurking on the river. However, finally they arrived in Hong Kong, whereupon Ralty left the Royal Navy - possibly this exploit had something to do with that - and joined the merchant fleet of Butterfield and Swire, a very big Hong Kong Hong$_{13}$. Swire traded over the whole of South East Asia from its base in Hong Kong to Australia, New Guinea, the Philippines and everywhere in between.

Auntie Mary's sadness was that they were unable to have children. It wasn't long before she'd roped Mother into volunteering at the Catholic Women's baby milk distribution centre in Wanchai. We called it The Milk Bar, because next door was the Pussycat Bar. Her secret agenda was to fall in love with an orphaned baby and inveigle Ralty into adopting one. Mum went with her to various orphanages I remember, but somehow it didn't happen. I went with them too, once. So Mary and Ralty ad hoc adopted me and to some extent my sisters instead. From about the age of twelve they took me on outings and to the cinema, and to smart grown-up dinners in places like Jimmy's Kitchen, where steaks were flambéed in brandy and cream, pudding was Baked Alaska, meals took hours and I couldn't keep my eyes open.

For some reason Auntie Mary's favourite outing was to the Tiger Balm Gardens in Happy Valley, famous for its winding paths, stylised arched Chinese bridges and colourful plants, but also for its fearsome pictures and statues of satanic imps torturing sinners for eternity in various grotesque ways. Catholic Mary thought this was fine, but it terrified me. It still does if I think about it.

Be that as it may, we were extremely fond of Auntie Mary. She had never lost her delight in dancing and parties, and sometimes she and Uncle Ralty took me and my parents to Saturday afternoon tea dances at the Shatin Heights Hotel. We used to sit at small tables set all around the elegant dance floor and eat little crustless cucumber, salmon or anchovy sandwiches, small chow such as curry puffs and tiny, colourful cakes.

There was an accomplished Palm Court band and Auntie Mary would be in devilish mood, fanning herself vigorously with her sandalwood fan and peering round the room for likely partners to torture me with. She would nudge me violently with her elbow, "Eh! Eh Mary! Look! He's nice! Ha ha!" and roll her eyes encouragingly.

I'd squeal with embarrassment at this of course and lurch away, "No! Don't!"

And she would laugh and poke me in the ribs with her folded fan. But sometimes it would be too late and she would catch a man's attention and I would be led off to be mortified on the dance floor... Although really I enjoyed it as she knew, and she also knew which of the young men were employed to dance with the ladies, so they were very kind to me.

Sometimes I had to pull myself together and dance properly with Uncle Ralty. He brooked no nonsense; you would be gripped firmly and dipped and turned in perfect time, so it looked from an observer's point of view as if you actually knew how to dance. Which was nice, though sadly mistaken.

Unfortunately, when I was older I was never invited to go to Nip's Dancing School with my parents, which I consider an example of supreme negligence, and I blame them completely for the fact that I've never been a good ballroom dancer. Though I can still dance the cha-cha after a fashion, since it was drummed into me by my dear Father. And we danced it together for the final time in London, at his ninetieth Christmas in 2008.

Auntie Mary, Auntie Marty having done her duty as Commodore's wife and given out the prizes.

THE INDOMITABLE MRS HSIEH AND THE
MANAGER OF THE WHOLE ESTATE

Mother and Auntie Mary met Mrs Hsieh when she was a young woman with a new baby daughter. She came to the Catholic Women's Mother and Baby Clinic in downtown Wan Chai, which was an unlikely place to have such a clinic, as anyone who knew Hong Kong in 1958 will tell you. It was known as the Baby Bar owing to its location. There was a narrow shop on one side selling rice of all sorts; beautiful basmati right down to grey sweepings, in delicious-smelling open hessian sacks presided over by a scrawny old man and a fat, fearsome ginger cat. It sat brooding, buddha-like, in the cockloft above the rice sacks watching for rodents, with eyes deceptively half closed.

On the other side of the clinic was the Pink Pussycat Bar and Nightclub, a notorious gathering place for American servicemen on Rest and Recreation from Vietnam and the British squaddies who went to drink and fight them on a Saturday night. Pairs of heavyweight US Military Police oversaw this weekly event. The squaddies, regular soldiers who were mainly Scots or Geordies, tended to be wiry, feral little men who had been fighting since the day they were born. The Americans however were mostly conscripts from the countryside who had been unable to escape to Canada to avoid being posted to Vietnam, and who didn't know where they were or why they were there. So it was an uneven battle in the main.

Auntie Mary was a mainstay of the Baby Bar, being a Catholic from Shanghai and thus speaking several Chinese dialects. She loved cuddling babies as she unfortunately had none of her own. My mother's Cantonese was not good at that time, but Mrs Hsieh decided to learn English and asked Mother to help her, which she happily said she would.

Her story was like many others but with a happier ending. She had been newly married and living in the countryside near Shanghai when she decided they should escape from China, in the maelstrom of Mao's Red Guards, during which forty million people died. On their way south, during the day the young Hsiehs hid in bushes, trekking only through the dark nights towards Guangzhou. It was very dangerous but eventually, exhausted, they reached the bay of Shenzhen.

They stole two black rubber inner tubes and a pump on their way, until finally they lowered these and themselves into the filthy bay at night and paddled the 4 kilometres across to Hong Kong waters. Somehow they evaded the Hong

Kong Marine Police launches which set out every night to catch illegal immigrants. They'd already defied the odds by not being torn to shreds by sharks and managing to evade the great, black, ocean-going Communist Chinese junks patrolling the seas to catch escapees for financial reward. Or to kill them. The sight of these junks with their red flags and cold-faced sailors sent shivers running down your spine.

Our admiration for Mrs Hsieh and her husband for surviving this knew no bounds. Refugees who made it to Hong Kong's shores were allowed to remain and she found a room for them both in a squatter hut on the hillside. She made a living by writing letters in her beautiful calligraphy for other refugees. Knowing life was risky and she'd better take her chances while the going was good, she had a baby; that is of course when my mother and Auntie Mary met her.

With diligent effort and by fair means or foul, she then managed to acquire a flat in a newly built estate of high rise resettlement blocks in Shaukiwan. And there she met her equal, her potential nemesis, The Manager Of The Whole Estate. I never knew the name of this blight on her entrepreneurial life, because she referred to him always in the whole six words. She regarded him as the nearest thing to God, just to consider such an august personage made her lower her voice in wonder.

However, in spite of the conundrum her awe

of this mighty personage presented her with, Mrs Hsieh was unerringly capitalistic and the flat was her pride and joy, not only because it housed her and Elizabeth - she had named her daughter after the Queen - and the much absent Mr Hsieh, but because at last she saw a source of regular income.

The flat was high up on the nineteenth floor. It had a bedroom, a main room with a corner kitchenette, a bathroom "with a bath!" as she exclaimed in delight, never having had one before, and a little balcony. She immediately saw the possibilities. Mrs Hsieh had a delightfully conspiratorial way of speaking and when she and my mother sat next to each other with their heads together Mrs Hsieh spoke in a throbbing, passionate voice about her plans.

"I don't need bedroom, of course," she scoffed, "who needs more than one room? Hah! I'm telling Cheung, the *secret room agent*, I am letting that whole bedroom! Soon I will have good money for this room! It is very nice room! Very clean!" she added, as if Mum was going to argue with her. There was always a fixer like Cheung in Hong Kong.

"But Mrs Hsieh, won't you get into trouble? You had to sign the lease just for your family? Not allowed lettings?"

Mrs Hsieh tossed her head. "How they find out? You tell them?" They both laughed and Mrs Hsieh banged Mum's knee in the Chinese way - you could hardly call it patting. A couple of weeks passed and then Mrs Hsieh phoned Mum to say she was very excited because a young and shrinking couple "too frighten to cause trouble, Mrs Mirra," had taken the room at a good price.

Mrs Hsieh's next project was to let out the balcony. This space was about four feet by seven feet and mainly used for drying clothes. However, she erected a wall of plywood along the front railings and covered the balcony with a makeshift canvas roof. A student, terrified of both the awesome Mrs Hsieh herself, and dread of what The Manager Of The Whole Estate might do to him if he found him, moved in. He slept on a camp bed and studied all night long by the light of a candle – all that Mrs Hsieh would allow him to use so as not to draw attention to himself.

Everything was going well until suddenly disaster struck, as Mrs Hsieh told Mum and Auntie Mary in dramatic fashion. She had had an unexpected argument with her downstairs neighbour about noise going on in the bedroom. As she said to my aunt and my mum, this was very surprising because the tenants in her bedroom looked so quiet and studious with their matching black-framed glasses. Who would have suspected they would be so frolicksome in bed?

The neighbour complained to The Manager Of The Whole Estate, who came himself to her flat! In person! He sternly warned her that sexy noises would not be tolerated, looking with predatory intent at pretty Mrs Hsieh. She sensed, she told Mum, that his interest had been piqued by these alleged noises and become more than simply official. She had had the foresight to shove the illegal couple under the bed when he rang the bell, because *the manager* then prowled around suspiciously, Mrs Hsieh said, eyes wide and hand to her chest with the excitement of it. But the couple remained silently quivering beneath the bed until eventually he went away.

The upshot of this was twofold; Mrs Hsieh now had The Manager's unwanted attention, and her letting business was under threat. The rumours and comings and goings were a constant drama in her - and thus Mother's - life. The student on the balcony graduated and left after a few months, and Mrs Hsieh decided to leave replacing him for a time, since various neighbours were now keen to report her and thus ingratiate themselves with The Manager. Who knows what they thought they would gain? It wasn't up to him to decide which flat anyone had, but any leverage was always good to have in Hong Kong.

Mrs Hsieh had met our multitude of animals whenever she came to visit Mum and describe to her with bated breath all the latest in her sagas of drama. Seeing our dog Wendy in particular she took it into her head that Elizabeth needed a dog - Auntie Mary had a dog too, everyone should have a dog! My mother tried to persuade her that a room on the nineteenth floor with a tiny balcony was not the place for a dog and then, fortunately, she saw our guinea pigs who lived in luxury on our large verandah. She decided Elizabeth should have a rabbit instead and she went off and bought a little white one. There were no animals allowed on the estate, but this small fact certainly didn't constrain Mrs Hsieh.

Since the student no longer occupied the shack on the balcony, the rabbit was ensconced there, in a little cage. Elizabeth cried that it was lonely, so the rabbit was allowed into their room, where of course it spread a trail of droppings. Mrs Hsieh was not having that. She decided to train the rabbit to use a cat litter tray. Much to Mother's amazement the rabbit agreed to be trained and lived a fat and lazy life hopping around the flat and using the litter tray without a mistake. This proceeded well for quite a while until one day The Manager dropped in unexpectedly, Mr Hsieh being out, and found the rabbit insolently asleep on the rug in the middle of the room.

Before he could threaten her regarding the no animals rule, Mrs Hsieh started shouting, "How did that rabbit get out of its cage?! Elizabeth, did you let it out? It is nearly fat enough to eat now! We shall have it tomorrow!" She told Mum he was highly suspicious but he said he would come tomorrow to try the rabbit stew she would make. So, hoist by her own petard$_{14}$ she had then to go to the market to buy some rabbit to cook and she coerced the now chastened couple in the bedroom to hide themselves, with Elizabeth's own fat rabbit in a large shoebox, under the bed again. Thus The Manager Of The Whole Estate was thwarted!

Mother didn't hear from Mrs Hsieh for a while, and we went on leave, so it wasn't until nearly nine months later that she burst once again into our lives. Mr Hsieh had left her! He had gone to Hawaii! One of her coterie of informants had told her because he had not said a word to Mrs Hsieh. Nobody could really blame him, he had long been the least of Mrs Hsieh's concerns as anyone reading this will have noticed. The luckless Mr Hsieh was hardly ever mentioned in his wife's life's melodrama.

She wanted a passport to go and look for him, she said, and she needed my dad, who as far as she was concerned was *the government*, to get one for her. Surprisingly enough Dad was indeed able to help her get a passport because one of his closest friends happened to be the Deputy

Director of Immigration.

The chaos and excitement around Mrs Hsieh going to Hawaii was terrific for a month or two, with Mother and Auntie Mary consulted every step of the way. How likely was the plane to stay in the sky? How did it stay in the sky? What food would you eat on the plane? Could you use a lavatory? Did you sleep in your pyjamas? Heaven knows what else Mrs Hsieh wanted to know!

Luckily the young couple renting the bedroom were not so young and naïve any more (nor so rampant) and they agreed to look after Elizabeth and see she went to school - as long as they could use the cooker in the main room instead of the tiny, one ring electric plate they had used all this time. She happily agreed. So off she went to Hawaii, where she had an address through a third party - only to discover Mr Hsieh had settled down in a spacious apartment and married an American.

She immediately phoned Mother from Hawaii and told her to instruct Father to write a letter to the President of the United States to inform him that Mr Hsieh was a bigamist and to send him home. Unfortunately, Dad wasn't quite as lofty in the government as she presumed and the letter was never written. When she returned to Hong Kong though, Dad did get his friend in Immigration to look at her Chinese marriage certificate, only to find it wasn't legitimate anyway...

Poor Mrs Hsieh, such a dire loss of face to be abandoned for a foreigner! But she invented an important and powerful job for Mr Hsieh, which kept him in America and through which she restored her confidence, and that perked her up no end. She elaborated on this job whenever she fancied, until she almost believed in it herself, and soon she had Mr Hsieh being driven around by a chauffeur and waited on by flunkies while eating T-bone steaks.

She decided to re-let the balcony and – even more exciting – she said that without her, now faux, husband splashing pee in the bathroom she could let that, too. A thin roadworker was stunned and delighted with his good fortune to be allowed to rent the bath. Mrs Hsieh put a couple of kapok mattresses[15] in the bath for him to sleep on. For the first time in his life, he said, he had privacy and a door to shut between himself and anyone else. And a toilet! Mrs Hsieh and Elizabeth used the toilet only when he was out at work – and the couple in the bedroom who needed to empty their potty and their water bowl did the same. Everyone was happy. Except for The Manager Of The Whole Estate, never able to prove his suspicions or snaffle Mrs Hsieh alone and wield his ignoble passions over her or catch her out in her illicit lettings.

My mother and Mrs Hsieh were friends for many years before our family left Hong Kong to much wailing and grief. Although Mum wrote to her, intrigued to know the latest exploits, after we left she didn't receive a reply. Mrs Hsieh was very good at moving on and move on she must have done, but not before she had given us the gift of some funny, bizarre and unforgettable memories.

TENT

On the left Mr KK So and Dad on the far right. They both look mischievous to me.

"I think we need a tent," declared Father. Mother looked up from her paper, alarmed.

"Really?"

"Tent! Tent!" cried my youngest sister and her annoying little friend, jumping up and down.

"Can we have a round tent with a pole in the middle?" I asked. "You know, you can ride your horse in?" I was eleven or so and keen on horses.

"Horses! Horses!" cried the little ones, galloping around the room and going "neigh".

"No, you're thinking about a circus tent Mary,

that's much too big."

"Are we going to the circus?" asked Trudi, wide-eyed.

"No! Now this is getting silly!" Dad put a roll of architect's paper on the table and spread it out, to show us his sketch of the putative tent.

"If you're going to jump on the sofa," said Mum, "will you please take your shoes off." The little ones kicked off their flip flops and renewed their bouncing.

"I've drawn a picture of it, come and see," said Dad. Obligingly, Mum got up and wandered over to the table, absentmindedly picking up the flip flops on the way. I looked, too. There was a large, rectangular tent with supporting legs in each corner, cross bars at the top and base and a backward-slanting roof to protect us from the elements, gaily striped and with a pretty scalloped edge in the front. Behind it he had sketched the mountains of Kowloon Peak.

Mother sat down to look at it more closely, idly picking up a pencil and drawing cartoon flowers and grass around the edges.

"Well, who would make it for us?" she asked.

"That's the marvellous thing!' said Dad with a beaming smile, "So K-K reckons his father-in-law could make the frame..."

The ubiquitous So Kar-Kiu was a great chum of his and they were often in cahoots with each other.

"Out of what?" asked Mum.

"Well... aluminium. He's got a factory. And also K-K says this chap will know someone to make the canvas tent as well. Isn't that lucky?!"

Ah Chun, in passing, leaned forward to have a look. She frowned. "What you put floor?"

Dad looked up at her, "Well, we won't have a floor Ah Chun! The idea is that this is a tent. For outside on the grass."

Ah Chun grimaced. "Ants," she said, disappearing through the kitchen door without another word. It banged behind her.

"Ants! Ants!" cried the little ones, jumping around waving their little anty arms.

"Hmmm! Not a popular idea there," remarked Mother, "are you quite sure we need this Harold? It's going to be awfully big and heavy to carry..."

"Not at all! And I thought green and white stripes? What do you think?"

"That sounds nice," said Mum. She drew a little bucket and spade to the side of Dad's illustration, and added a cartoon signpost saying "Beach".

So Kar-Kiu was as good as his word. He and Dad drew up the measurements before K-K got in touch with his father-in-law. Both being chartered surveyors, it was a fun project for them I'm sure. And I can imagine the factory workers' comments when they saw Mum's pretty additions to Dad's sketch, they being so literal and scathing like all Chinese working men,

"This is a tent."

"Yes. It is a Foreign Devil's tent."

"But there is grass around it. It is for going on grass."

"If the Devils want to go on the grass, why not? Let them sit on the grass!"

"Ha ha ha." Uproarious laughter.

"But look, there is a bucket."

"This arrow says 'beach' in their writing."

"But this is in mountains."

"Those gweilos[16] are stupid! There is no beach in the mountains."

"Who can understand those people? They are not like us."

Agreement all round.

Even Father was slightly aghast when the finished product arrived at the office and he and the office clerks staggered about loading it into the car. The mighty aluminium struts and cross bars were contained in four canvas bags. In another bag the heavy green and white canvas tent was hard to handle, too. Some of the men downstairs at our flat helped him bring everything up and the next thing I remember was all of it lying on the old hall rug, beside the dogs and their bones.

"Mary, pick up that end," Dad said to me. I looked at the section he was pointing at. "I can't," I said, without trying.

"Come on! It's not that heavy! Just pick it up!"

I bent down gingerly and picked it up. It was

in fact heavier than I'd expected so I dropped it forthwith and it banged down onto the rug, fortunately, because it could have hit the parquet floor and damaged it. Dad rolled his eyes.

Mother took pity on me and lifted it and they carried it and all the other various parts into one of the spare amah's rooms. Mother, having been a Land Girl and a great tennis player, was so much stronger than she looked. So there was the tent in all its glory, lying in the room beside Ah Chun's bedroom and no doubt receiving caustic comments from the amahs like, "They'll never use that tent."

But they were wrong! The following Saturday we packed up a celebratory cold chicken and lemon meringue pie picnic – although Ah Chun was against the pie, envisaging an army of ants consuming all in their path, including us – and we set off for Kowloon Peak. Not for the faint-hearted was the challenge of loading the tent into the back of the car. Father eventually discarded about half of the framework as unnecessary and removed the heavy, long base bars as well as the brace joints at the top, so we were left with a slimline edition. The way K-K's father-in-law had built it, it would have withstood any weather, as if people were going to sip wine and munch cocktail snacks in the middle of a typhoon, but it was a lighter version we pushed into the boot and tied down with rope. The large folded canvas tent made a chair on the back seat for little Sally. She was thrilled. She could see out of the window for once.

It was an excursion to get to Kowloon by car in those days. We had to drive to the Yau Ma Tei car ferry in Western first, since the Cross-Harbour Tunnel was not even a dream then. There was always a long, hot wait for the ferry, only made bearable by the ice cream sellers with their freezer boxes on the front of their bicycles. Mother liked classic Dairy Farm ice cream cones but I loved Beanos, frozen Chinese red-lotus-bean soup on sticks, from the purple-coloured bicycles of On Lok Yuen$_{17}$. I also liked fried, bright orange baby octopus on sticks but eating those in the car was a step too far for Mother. We played I spy until boarding and hearing the weird announcement, so amplified and distorted no-one knew what it meant, "Wa wa na nee, wo wo, wa nee!"

Once in Kowloon we trailed through packed back streets to Nathan Road and finally, upward to the mountains! It was lovely, Dad was right. The view was spectacular. Dad hummed as they put the tent together while we intermittently did handstands. Finally, it was up! Mother laid out a tablecloth and artistically arranged our picnic upon it and we all sat down within its shelter. Mother handed out plates and serviettes and there we were, in our tent.

The first thing we noticed was how hot it

was. The sun blazed down on the canvas. Then next – Ah Chun's ants. All the many types of ant in Hong Kong appeared to have gathered on Kowloon Peak for a performance of The Big Ant Show. We were a mecca for the entire ant population, including large red biting ants with claws like crabs. Ten abreast they marched over Mother's tablecloth towards the chicken, until they noticed moments later the lemon meringue pie and veered purposefully towards it. Mother whipped it off the grass and ran with it back to the car. Without a word we removed the salads, bread and everything else from the tent and loaded it into the car, then sat on the hot leather seats to eat our picnic.

"Never mind Dad," we all said, "it's a lovely tent, it will be fantastic in winter!"

"We certainly won't get wet if it rains, darling," said Mum staunchly.

So we went for a walk around the hill, came back, dismantled the tent, drove down the mountain and went to the beach. And on that beach and many others, the tent came into its own! A wonderful ant-free room, somewhere to get out of the wind and weather, somewhere private to lie down in... For several years we had a lot of fun in the tent, as Dad had known we would. My sisters and I well remember all the times we staggered around hauling bits of tent up and down paths and clambering over rocks trying to reach Dad's designated perfect spot. It was an indestructible tent. A tent for the ages. I wish I knew what had happened to it.

LESSONS

"Missee!" hissed Ah Chun from the doorway of my parent's bedroom. Mother looked up from the mass of pink netting that she was battling with at her sewing machine; she was making a fairy costume, also involving pink satin wings and glitter.

"Missee – Japan lady come!"

"Oh blast! She's early!" exclaimed Mother, leaping up.

"She Japan dress!" declared Ah Chun excitedly, her eyes gleaming.

"What's going on?" I asked. I was lying on my parent's bed indulging in my favourite pastime, talking.

"It's a Japanese lady who's come for some English lessons," Mother revealed as she went to the mirror above the fireplace to tidy her hair and dab on some lipstick. Then she hurried with Ah Chun out to the hall.

"You stay here Mary," she said over her shoulder as I, obviously, followed them out.

There, on our faded and battered old rug by the front door stood a perfect, doll-like Japanese lady in full costume. She was wearing a beautiful white and black patterned kimono fastened with a white obi belt, her gleaming black hair was piled on her head and held in place with glossy red sticks, and on her feet, split socks with blocky wooden shoes. She wore white make-up and had cherubic red lips and black-lined eyes. Ah Chun and I gasped delightedly. She looked tiny in contrast to the blond American standing beside her in his white Naval uniform.

As Mother approached, the Japanese lady bowed from her waist, hands clasped in front of her and whispered, "Haarro Teecha". Fortunately, Mother knew to bow back, and then after a moment to rise before the lady as she was the superior in this instance. If she had not, the lady could have remained doubled over permanently.

"Captain Beckwith?" enquired Mother, shaking hands.

"This is my wife, Mrs Beckwith," the American said glowing with pride. Mrs Beckwith smiled shyly. Mother ushered them into the dining room and I curled into an adjacent balcony chair so I could listen to their conversation. Glancing up, I saw Mrs Beckwith's eyes alight with pleasure as she sat opposite Mother at the big dining table.

"Could you give me some background, Captain?" asked Mum. "I believe your wife doesn't speak any English at all?"

"No, we've lived in Japan for ten years, until now," he replied. "We met through a programme set up by our governments and she's not been out of Japan before, but now I've been posted to Hong Kong and really, she has to learn a little English to communicate with anybody!"

Then he spoke in Japanese quickly to his wife, who nodded and beamed at Mum.

"I'm looking forward to teaching her! But why haven't you taught her yourself?"

"Well," replied the Captain, "I want her to have an English accent. You see," he continued, leaning forward conspiratorially, "Asian ladies with American accents can be mistaken for – er – 'companions' rather than wives. I would prefer her to speak like you, Mrs Miller, with a proper English accent so nobody will ever misjudge her."

In 1961 it was true that Asian women with American sailors were often thought, cynically, to have sold themselves but even so Mum was rather taken aback by this.

She had had a lot of experience teaching kindergarten children but this was her first foray into teaching adults. She'd been asked by a Japanese member of her Club if she would give these lessons and since Dad was planning a three-month-long worldwide trip for us all on our next leave, during which Mother felt she might require a considerable amount of spending money, she had agreed to take it on.

She had a simple plan. To teach as small children learn, so she'd prepared a set of pictures of familiar things to teach Mrs Beckwith their names. But first, she pressed her hand to her chest and declared, "I am Mrs Miller!"

She gestured to the Japanese lady to do the same and said, "I am Mrs Beckwith," and encouraged her to repeat this, "I am Mrs Beckwit," she said.

"Mrs Beckwith."

"Mrs Beckwit." Mum nodded and smiled.

"Am I Mrs Beckwith?" asked Mother, pointing to herself, shaking her head and saying, "No".

Mrs Beckwith laughed and shook her head, too.

"No! I am Mrs Beckwit!" she said.

On they went until Mrs Beckwith had agreed that the dog was not Mrs Beckwith, nor was the chair, the table, Captain Beckwith or a giant fern...

Mother spread her flash cards all over the table. "Ball," she said, pointing at the card.

"Ball," repeated Mrs Beckwith. They covered the table with pictures and named them, then Mum turned them all over and Mrs Beckwith had to turn them up one by one and identify them. She was in hysterics and we couldn't help laughing with her as she lurched from one to the other grabbing them and guessing the words while her husband watched her enjoying the challenge.

Over the years Mrs Beckwith became an institution in our house. Once a week she arrived, never again in full regalia sadly but always happy, and her English improved rapidly. Through her, Mother acquired another Japanese student, Mr Yoshida, whom Mrs Beckwith had met at a club for Japanese citizens. He was a glum, unsmiling man who was a manager in a Japanese emporium called Daimaru$_{18}$, whose headquarters had instructed him to improve his schoolboy English.

While Mrs Beckwith giggled and learned effortlessly, Mr Yoshida was so self-conscious he found it hard to say anything in case he was wrong, particularly to a woman. So, for Mum it was like communicating with a disobliging rock. However, Mother's relentless charm (through gritted teeth) eventually won over Mr Yoshida and he and Mrs Beckwith teamed up to bring us children presents of great extravagance every Christmas and Easter, though they knew nothing then about the meaning of either.

The first was an unforgettable chocolate Easter Chicken. Its box was a gaudy pink, arrayed with huge-eyed cartoon chicks and so large Mr Yoshida struggled to carry it up to our flat. Inside, behind a cellophane window, brooded the Chicken of Chickens, dark and vast, with red claws and a fat chocolate body, a baleful eye staring terrifyingly up at us over its sharp yellow beak.

"Goodness! You shouldn't have!" exclaimed Mother as my little sister ran sobbing in fright from it.

Mrs Beckwith, as ever, was excited, "Now you must smash chicken for Happy Easter!" she cried happily, "Smash smash!"

"Yes, indeed," Mother replied, while Mr Yoshida grimaced an Oriental smile.

"It is best chicken from my company, Daimaru," he stated, "Japanese chocolate is best chocolate. Daimaru is best shop. This is very expensive chicken. Your husband, children, even you may enjoy." He bowed.

Mother smiled her best smile. "Oh we will!" she exclaimed. "My husband will be SO pleased! And I also," she added pointedly.

Later, we ate some of it. It was strangely grainy, and very, very sweet but Ah Chun loved it. As we all said to her, just eat as much as you want. Or can.

The chicken of chickens was followed over the years by many Easter animals - a selection of ferocious Easter bunnies wth huge teeth in particular. Perhaps the most peculiar was the Easter giraffe, resplendent in an unwieldy orange and black striped velvet box about four feet long. It was obviously Daimaru's finest and most expensive chocolate giraffe, created by Japan's most gifted chocolate makers and only available to Mr Yoshida of Daimaru department store. Lucky us.

After this first meeting with Mrs Beckwith I had to go to my dreaded tennis lesson.

Mother was a good player herself and couldn't believe I wouldn't be, but sadly for her I was terrible, mainly because I so rarely connected with the ball. So I said goodbye to the Beckwiths and set off in my white shorts and Aertex shirt and wandered sadly to the Peak Tram, to take it halfway down to May Road. It was like being in the country. Birds and butterflies, sometimes centipedes and lizards distracted me as I walked disconsolately towards my nemesis – Mr Eduardo "Eddie" da Sousa, the tennis coach, for my fourth abortive lesson. I was the epitome of misery when I reached the steps down to the tennis courts. There stood Mr da Sousa, about as happy to see me as I was him.

"Hello Mr da Sousa," I said.

He rolled his eyes and sighed. "Hello Mary. Are we planning to try and hit the ball today?"

"I always try," I replied, stung, "it's just that I don't know which hand to use."

"We've had this conversation! Other ambidextrous people manage fine! We agreed, Mary! You'd use your right hand for backhand and both hands for forehand balls."

"Oh, yes."

"So let's have some gentle shots to start with and then see if we can play a little game, shall we, since that's why you're here?" he added sarcastically, bouncing a few balls hard with his racquet.

Advancing scarily towards me and the net,

he batted a ball at me. I watched it. I tried. My mind went blank. Which hand? Which hand? I ducked as the ball whizzed past me. He tried again. I tried again, then eventually shut my eyes and flailed out in the direction of the ball and hit it! It went over the net and Mr da Sousa whacked it back, whereupon it hit my knee. I prayed for this agony to end, as did he, and then our prayers were answered. Mother walked through the gate.

I have rarely seen a more relieved expression on anyone's face than that on Eddie da Sousa's at the sight of Mother. Her flouncy little tennis skirt set off her tanned legs and her white blouse had a cornflower blue collar, matching her eyes. She waved her tennis racquet in greeting before rolling a sweat band over her golden hair.

"Oh Mrs Miller!" breathed Mr da Sousa as she walked towards me and took my racquet away.

"You go and sit in the shade darling," she said tenderly, "it's not fair to make you do this. Here," and she got my current book out of her bag, "I brought your book. You go and read."

Never have I loved her more – probably that was true of Mr da Sousa, too – as she smiled and handed me my book.

Then she put everything on a bench, took up her racquet and did some little bouncy steps and whack! Mr da Sousa had a tennis game and I sat in a corner, soothed by the steady thwack of balls and squeak of tennis shoes not involving me. Hooray.

Lesson of the day I thought as we drove home, you don't have to be good at everything, people who matter will love you anyway.

CAPTAIN BECKWITH'S STORY

Over the years Mother got to know Captain Beckwith's history and how he came to live and work in Japan and marry Mrs Beckwith.

Chester Philips Beckwith was named after his great uncle who had been a confederate general in the American civil war. He was born on December 2, 1922 in Virginia - the last, and as he said himself, a late, unexpected and unfortunately unwanted addition to a high flying family. His father served in the Pentagon in some capacity; he never knew precisely what he did but the remuneration seemed magnificent, though it meant he was rarely at home.

His two much older brothers were away at the military Randolph-Macon Academy in Virginia so baby Chester was home by himself most of the time, particularly as his mother, as a member of an old aristocratic family of West Virginia and thus a Daughter of the American Revolution, was required to perform the duties of a society hostess. This meant arranging concerts and charity auctions, which pulled in a great deal of money for endowments, and at which all the great and the good had to be seen.

Originally, Chester was left in the loving and capable hands of his nanny, Mammy Rosa, a black lady of traditional proportions, who had worked for the Beckwiths for a number of years. However, sadly Rosa was hit by a chauffeur-driven car in downtown Savannah, Georgia, while visiting relatives and was killed. Her death incidentally seemed never to have been fully investigated and Captain Beckwith never discovered who it was who'd owned the car and had been sitting in the back.

This meant that fifteen month old Chester was alone in the big, colonial house, apart from the cook and a couple of maids. What happened then was to influence his whole life. At the time, Japanese émigrés worked in America in fair numbers, mainly as gardeners, and the Beckwiths employed a Japanese gardener, too, whose wife helped him by working with him in the garden. She saw the young maids trying to cope with the baby and instinctively picked him up, cuddled him and cared for him. She was in her mid thirties at the time. As soon as Mrs Beckwith Sr heard about this she was extremely relieved and employed Sakura Nakajima as his nanny on the spot.

Thus it was that Chester's first language was actually Japanese. He played and grew and became just like Sakura and her husband Haru; their little blond son. They taught him the Japanese way of doing things and it was, he said, very hard for him indeed when he started school soon after his fifth birthday and had to learn how to be an American boy. Chester continued his close relationship with the Nakajima's faithfully throughout his life.

The Beckwiths did not suffer during the Great Depression it seems, and life apparently went on fairly smoothly until war was declared in Europe. The Beckwiths, like most very wealthy folk in the USA, were well invested in arms manufacture so the war had a beneficial economic impact on them, and they managed to keep their two older sons out of it too by getting them government jobs. Then came Pearl Harbour and suddenly Haru and Sakura were rounded up, together with over one hundred and fifty thousand other Japanese, and put in concentration camps.

By this time Chester had finished a year at the Naval Academy in Annapolis, Maryland himself. One day a big black government car flying the Stars and Stripes swooped into the college driveway and a captain arbitrarily scooped him up from the academy and took him to one of these Japanese internment camps. There were almost no white Americans at the time who spoke perfect Japanese, and he found himself suddenly becoming a naval lieutenant in charge of interpreting the inmates. The distress the Japanese internees felt was a body blow to Chester.

"But we are American citizens!" he heard, over and over again. He did his best to convey not just their words but their emotions, their disillusion and their humiliation to their American *jailers*, for want of a better word. It was a bitter reward to be promoted because of his ability to explain and negotiate between the Japanese and the Americans, when he himself was both.

After the war, when Japan had surrendered and the Americans established themselves in Tokyo, it was obvious that Chester would be posted there to help liaise – and one evening at a cultural exchange in Kyoto he met his love, his wife, the lively and beautiful Mrs Beckwith, friend of my mother.

EASTER ON THE MOUNTAIN

After Christmas, Easter was the next big thing on our calendar.

Before dawn on Easter Sunday we were woken up. It was always cold, and the mist hung thickly around our building; it was the season for mist.

Quietly, my sister Trudi and I got dressed and joined Dad in the car to drive up to the top of Mount Austin, the highest point on the Peak, where there was a little garden and a squat stone building. Several people would be there waiting for us in the dark. The men would manhandle the small Hammond organ out of the back of one of the cars and place it carefully where they thought the sound would carry best, because the wind always got up just around dawn.

Dad brought his piano stool over, sat down and started to pump the slightly squeaky foot pedals to warm up the organ, then he played a few bars to test it. The notes sounded melancholy in the pre-dawn darkness. He left his hymnal on the organ stand and joined the other men at the stone storage shed.

More people arrived and gathered together, pulling their jackets around themselves and stamping their feet up and down to keep warm. Soon I would have to take my cold hands out of my pockets to turn the pages of the music. In the meantime someone erected a blackboard with the hymn numbers chalked on it, and wedged it with large stones so that it wouldn't blow away.

The men took the base plinth out of the shed and carried the heavy lump of concrete over to the edge of the site, placing it exactly east. Dawn was about to break. They returned to the shed and carefully lifted out the massive wooden cross. There was no body on it, it was a plain, empty cross, about twelve feet tall. They carried it to the plinth and with some effort adjusted its base so that it would slide into the slot in the plinth. Then they pulled on the ropes they'd wrapped around it and heaved it upright.

Dad sat down at the organ. You could hear his feet pumping the wheezy foot pedals to bring the organ to life. The sun was just about to rise; beams of light appeared low on the horizon behind the cross illuminating it so that it stood out starkly in the dissipating mist. Slowly the sun rose. Dad started the introduction to the first verse of the first hymn and the congregation sang as it grew lighter. The cross stood out as a black shape against the rising sun, mist drifting around it. It was an intense and emotional time; more so as the little organ's notes ebbed and flowed in the strong dawn breeze and the people's voices faded in and out, so the singing sounded ethereal.

I stood beside Dad turning the pages. I sang along too as I knew all these Easter hymns, their special meaning, their passion and their joy. Christ our Lord is risen today, Hallelujah.

The little service didn't last long. With a great flourish Dad pumped extra hard and the organ wheezed out its last few, triumphant notes. Dad played the final chord. Now the sun had risen above the cross, the mist was almost gone, it was getting warmer and it was time to pack up and leave.

There were a few women there, but most had instead gone to the church hall to get the Easter breakfast ready. Long tables were laid out with pretty yellow gingham cloths, and the hard boiled eggs, all highly coloured by various groups of children over the previous day, sat in their bowls along the tables. There were rolls and hot cross buns and sausages, orange juice and toast.

Once the cross and the plinth had been stowed safely away, we drove back down from Mount Austin to collect Mother and Sally and go on down the Peak to the church where we would meet everyone for breakfast. After that we would all go home and take off our jeans and sweaters, and put on our Easter attire. Those were the days of pretty full skirts, high heeled shoes, and hats. The church would be full and the Easter hymns would ring out in celebration.

Eating breakfast together was nice and we

were hungry after our very early morning. But the effect the mountain and the cross had on me was momentous every year, so I was withdrawn and quiet at breakfast and wanted to go home. The picture in my mind of a man hanging in dreadful pain on a cross for hours or days haunted me. The actual-sized cross darkly outlined by the rising sun seemed to summarise the paradox of good and evil on our earth.

I needed to go home. I was so greatly grieved by the cruelty of mankind.

MR SUBINDAR SINGH

The doorbell rang and our amah Ah Chun answered it. "Missee!" she bellowed, "Indian man here." If my mother had not been at home, Ah Chun would have slammed the door in his face. She distrusted men in general but more than that, she was very protective of Mother and was convinced that hordes of unsavoury men were lining up to take advantage of her good nature.

Fortunately for him, Mother was in the house and politely greeted the man as he stood in our hall. He bowed, his mighty burgundy turban bent low, and then he whipped out a calling card printed in gold on a background of maroon from his voluminous pocket and presented it to her.

"I am Mr Subindar Singh, Madam, and I have many beautiful rugs and carpets to show you please, all very special price and perfectly suitable for your home Madam," he said, showing his gleaming white teeth in the depths of his elegant black beard and moustache.

"Well, I'm not..." began Mother uncertainly.

"I will show you just some and you will see for yourself how beautiful!"

"Err..." replied Mother not wanting to be rude, but she had hesitated and thus was lost.

Mr Subindar Singh signalled through the open front door to the two lugubrious coolies who were waiting on the landing with rolls of carpets slung over their shoulders. Ah Chun was standing in the kitchen doorway observing this, on guard to protect Mum from all comers. She frowned at the coolies as they picked their way warily past her and around the dogs, who were lying haphazardly about like a canine obstacle course, and lowered their burdens to the floor. Ah Chun glowered at them and they scuttled back to sit on the cool stone steps of the stairwell. She nearly closed the front door on their feet as they went.

Mr Singh began to strut over to the first roll of carpets the coolies had lain on the parquet floor of the music room. But unfortunately before he had gone two steps, he tripped over a couple of the dogs' bones lying on the rug in the hallway. He staggered sideways, almost impaling himself on Dad's music stand, spun around and in so doing, his eye fell on the hall rug itself. For a long moment there was silence as he gathered his breath, then slowly he turned back to stare at Mum.

"From where did you get this rug, Madam?" he asked in a strangulated voice.

"My father gave it to me actually," replied Mum, slightly confused, whereupon Mr Singh dug around in his bag and produced a sheaf of well thumbed papers, stapled together, and shuffled through them. Finally, he found the one he wanted and showed it to Mum.

"This is very important rug, Madam, very important! You see! See the picture, the pattern? It is very old, from 1800! My goodness me, many people are looking hither and thither for this rug!"

He wiped his face with a sparkling white handkerchief, quite overwhelmed.

Alarmed, Ah Chun swiftly picked up the dogs' bones and called our wash amah, Ah Oi, to come with a brush and dustpan. Ah Oi hurried in and started sweeping the bits of bone and general detritus off the now, apparently, much sought after and valuable article.

Mr Singh bent and lifted the corner of the rug to see the faded, handwritten details on the label beneath. He read out the number and then checked it again. He sighed. Ah Oi took the brush and dustpan away and Ah Chun carried the offending bones into the dining room, the dogs obediently following her.

"It is very sad that this rug is neglected," he said, shaking his head.

I had been listening to this conversation from my room, and now the temptation to join in overtook me. Soon, standing side by side, Ah Chun and I both stared at the rug, the very rug which we had been using as a doormat and on which I rubbed my feet free of the filth of downtown Hong Kong on a daily basis, when I returned from my marathon school journey. It looked no different than it always had – a bit threadbare, intricately patterned in faded blue and pink.

"What should we do about it?" I asked.

"It must be cleaned! I shall clean it very well for you! And then I shall bring back to you this wonderful carpet with brass rings and a beautiful brass rail to hang it on the wall."

"That would be nice," said Mum faintly. I could see she was feeling overcome. She sat down hard on the piano stool.

"But Madam, from where did your father find this rug?"

"I suppose he had it in London. He was an antique dealer, you know."

"And I'm thinking, does he know this is where the dogs are chewing their bones, on this very rug, Madam?"

Mum jumped guiltily. "Well, I have never actually mentioned it, I suppose," she said.

Ah Chun hurried over and stood beside her. "You not worry missee!" she said stoutly, "plenty more rug."

Mum smiled at her.

Meanwhile Mr Subindar Singh had regained

his aplomb. "So, I will take it to clean. And now we look at another one to replace, but not for dogs!" he declared, opening the front door and beckoning in one of the coolies, who rolled up our erstwhile doormat rug and took it outside. Mr Singh wrote an elaborate description of it in his sales docket book and tore it out to give to Mother, and swiftly started unrolling the first bundle of carpets.

Soon the floor was covered in the most colourful and beautiful display I had ever seen. He had not been exaggerating, indeed he had a spectacular collection: Indian, Persian, Turkish and Afghani rugs in wool and silk, a feast for the eyes. They flooded over the waxed wooden floor of the big music room, under the grand piano and coming to rest eventually against the organ. I longed to walk on them as Mr Singh was encouraging me to do, but Mother glanced at my filthy feet so I rushed off to wash them in the nearest bathroom, which happened to belong to my sisters. Unfortunately, I had forgotten the bath was full of terrapins with their various objects of delight - flat rocks, pebble mountains, plastic iguanas - so I had to hoick my feet up into the washbasin, but never mind, I was soon back and walking on these beautiful treasures. How soft and silky some felt, how deep and knotty, others!

Mr Singh wrung his hands in pleasure as he watched me fall in love with his rugs. His coolies were dispatched down to his van again and again, carrying more and more rugs up to lay upon the floor. Finally, I chose one above others, a delicate, smooth, shining blue with a beautiful pale pattern all around the edges and an intricate weaving of animals in the centre. "Oh, I love this one!" I exclaimed.

"Young lady, you have made a very clever and excellent choice!" He shook his head in appreciation while Mother's face blanched. "That is very old. It is silk. It is the most expensive carpet I have here, very precious...!"

Mother gulped desperately, "Ermm, I don't think..."

Mr Singh smiled tenderly at her. "No, I think not that one for you today, Madam!"

Looking grateful, Mother roamed around the carpets. Eventually, she chose a small Turkish rug with vibrant dark colours on a deep, sky blue background. The coolies started to roll all the rugs up again, under the eagle eye of Ah Chun, who didn't trust them any further than she could throw them. Mr Singh wrote another long docket full of numbers, and Mum paid him. Then off he and his retinue went, tenderly carrying our erstwhile dog mat and Mum and I collapsed into the rattan chairs on the verandah, exhausted.

The estimable Mr Subindar Singh visited our apartment about once a year. Mother built up quite a collection of carpets of every colour and size. Now our supposedly valuable ex-doormat hangs from its rings on its brass rail in my sister Trudi's hallway. As I write, I have my feet resting on the huge, highly patterned, scarlet Persian carpet that had lain under our parents' dining table for all the following years wherever they lived, in Hong Kong, Gibraltar and Cornwall.

Now it's lying on my own sitting room floor shining its bright colours up at me, bringing with them the warm heart of our childhood home.

LIVING IN THE SHADOW OF MAO'S CHINA

It was soon after my thirteenth birthday that Father asked me to come and have a chat with him in his study. I sat in the chair next to his desk staring out of the window, thinking about how a bunch of us had played spin the bottle on the roof of our flats the previous night and wondering if we were going to do it again this night. I was relishing the thrilling, closed-mouth touch of Johnny's soft lips on mine when he had kissed me in the semi-darkness behind the chimney stacks...

"Mary, are you listening to me?" asked Dad.

No I wasn't. "Yes," I said.

"I think you're old enough to learn how everything runs in this house..." he started.

I thought, oh no I am not! And, I don't want to, thank you! He opened a beige cardboard file that was on his desk, full of sheets of paper covered with his tiny, tidy writing. How come Dad was so neat, I wondered idly...

"Come on darling, you have to concentrate!" he said.

"Sorry."

"What I want to say and I want you to understand, is that if something were to happen to your mother and me, you would be in charge."

What?

"What do you mean?" I asked.

"Well, Mum and I don't want you girls split up. If something happened…"

"What do you mean *if something happened*?"

I could see he was finding me difficult. I might have been the oldest by almost four years, but I was still young and he pulled himself together.

"If Mum and I had something… an accident…"

"Oh," I said, frowning.

"I want to explain what you would have to do. And I want you to listen, please, because this is important!"

"All right." I wriggled on my chair, nervously.

"Now then. You girls are not to be split up. You understand? You are not to allow anyone at all to take your sisters somewhere without you. You are in charge."

Cold shivers ran down my spine. Who would take my sisters away from me?

"Grandad's in Canada and Nana's in Rhodesia so it has to be up to you. You see?"

I was looking uncomfortable.

He went on, "So we want you to take the girls to England, to the house there."

I returned to staring out of the window. I couldn't take it in. The house in England. I didn't like the house in England. It seemed impossible.

How could I go so far away with my sisters; the youngest was only five? I couldn't carry all the suitcases. I couldn't imagine going to England. I didn't know anything about England. I hated the thought of the house in England anyway - Mother always cried from the minute she got to that house until the minute we left to come home.

"Will you please stop fiddling with my pencil box," Dad said.

I had been sliding the top of his wooden pencil box backwards and forwards in an intensely irritating way. It helped me to think.

"Dad, I don't want to go to England."

"No, but you will have to, because you will have to go to Auntie Brenda." I knew my father's older sister, Auntie Brenda. "And she lives in England."

I nodded, "Well what about the tickets?"

"Mrs MacKenzie at Jardines will organise that, she always does our tickets. But before that, here is everything you have to do first." He opened a black and gold tin box with a little key. Inside it there were what seemed like an astonishing amount of red Hong Kong five hundred dollar bank notes, rolled up and neatly bound in elastic bands, with handwritten notes attached to them.

"This is very important. These are the ones for Ah Chun and Ah Oi. You have to give them their money. They must be paid, that is the highest priority. They must not be left without money. It would be very dangerous for them."

"Okay." This seemed self-evident, frankly.

"I'm going to talk to Ah Chun soon and she'd help you to pack and that sort of thing. Because this flat will have to be emptied. You know it's a government flat."

"But Dad, this is not going to happen!"

I looked away from the window, back through his study door and into the vast area which was our flat. With its huge reception area for parties, it had a music room, a sitting room, a dining room, four bedrooms, three bathrooms, a study, two verandahs, a kitchen, a pantry, eight rooms for the amahs, a servants' back landing, the washroom and their bathroom. And a walk-in hot cupboard. And everywhere was full of everything; pianos, ornaments, dolls, three piece suites. My heart sank to my boots.

"What am I supposed to do with it all Dad?" I moaned. I was near tears. He laid a neat, handwritten piece of paper down in front of me.

"Don't get all melodramatic, darling," he soothed. "Here is a list of all the addresses and phone numbers you would need – you just telephone Mr Yu at Yu San Kee Removals and they'll come and box everything up and ship it to England. Not the government furniture, of course," he added hastily. At least I knew not the government furniture, the enormously heavy, immovable, unbreakable teak furniture that government employees had supplied to them.

"Now," he said brightly. "Some bills will need attention – and here's the cheque book. I've made it really easy for you darling, I've written in the companies that will need paying and signed the cheques, and all you have to do is fill in the amounts and the date – here - when the bills come in. Look – here's China Light and Power, for instance. And here's Rediffusion. You just get the bill and complete the amount, like this..." His voice faded away.

I was staring at him, aghast. Was this real? Was this to do with the craziness going on in China? Was Dad thinking that he might be killed if the Chinese came over the border, which they were always threatening to do? Would the Gurkhas at the border, however brave they were and however scary the Chinese soldiers found them, really be able to hold back so many? And the Scots scared them too with their kilts and their bagpipes, but there were so few of them! And Dad in his Auxiliary Marine Police boat up at the border with the armed communist junks? And what could possibly happen to Mum?

Something made me look at him closely. It was as if I could suddenly see him through different eyes; as if I had never seen him before and I understood this strange conversation was making him deeply distressed. Furthermore, I didn't believe a word he'd said. I took a deep breath to remonstrate with him when he sighed and shut his file.

"It's all too much. I know," he said. It seemed the energy drained from him. I felt such an intense emotion at seeing him so downcast, probably for the first time.

"No, it's all right Dad, I'll manage," I said hastily, almost believing it for a moment.

He sighed. He closed the tin box and, briefly, his eyes. "It won't come to that," he said.

"No."

"But at least you know what to do. Don't you?"

"Yes."

He blew his nose on his hanky, pushed his chair back and stood up, fluffing my hair. "Come on then," he said. "Let's go and have lunch now."

BOATING WITH OUR FATHER

Our father was a man of many enthusiasms. His mantra was, "Whatever you do, it's got to be fun!" and he lived by this guiding principle all his life, even in North Africa during the war. While shaping up to do battle with Rommel he joined a civilian band, was adopted by a devoted Syrian family after whose youngest daughter I am named, and played his trombone jauntily in venues all over Cairo.

Boating with our father.
Here is Thea without Dora and Dad fiddling with something.

We grew up with this *fun* maxim of his and

his unshakeable belief that everything would work out fine. And it usually did, even though sometimes in spite of his endeavours rather than because of them, and this was particularly true of our excursions in boats.

Dad did not grow up with boats. The closest he'd got to boating was rowing around the Serpentine in Hyde Park. However, all male employees in the government were, somewhat ironically, required to volunteer in one of the auxiliary forces part-time, with a paid, two week full-time stint every year, in defence of the realm. Having had enough of the army after five years of war, he joined the Auxiliary Marine Police. He looked dashing in his cap and his seafaring uniform, especially his navy blue woollen Guernsey sweater, which was quite tight and which I borrowed whenever I could get my hands on it. Although this was an unpopular move as I grew older - as Dad plaintively said, he felt a bit of a fool standing there with the crew in a fully fashioned jumper, courtesy of Maidenform$_{19}$ cross your heart bras.

He didn't take long to fall in love with boats however, and had in mind a perfect little motorboat. Not a sailboat; neither of our parents had a clue how to sail and Mum was not a great swimmer. I don't think she was a massively keen boater either, but who could bear to gainsay Dad?

They were great friends with a Scottish couple called Eva and Alec and the four of them bought a small boat with a double cabin, to use together in the week and on alternate weekends. They called her Thea, for Thelma, Harold, Eva and Alec. She trailed a dory they called Dora. I thought this was brilliantly clever – Theadora! But I was young then and easily impressed.

So began our adventures on Thea. When we arrived at Aberdeen Harbour around the back of Hong Kong island where Thea was moored, I used to go and flop in sun-drenched indolence on Thea's cabin roof on a lilo, sweating and listening to the top one hundred on my transistor radio, which featured such songs as *Oh Carol*, *Sealed With A Kiss*, and of course the notorious *Yellow Polka Dot Bikini*. Mum read the paper and my sisters played while Dad got on with the multiple vital things that you appear to have to do with boats before you can set off.

First, he had to get the two-stroke mixture for the engine, so he trotted about with plastic containers for a while. Then there were adjustments to be made and something like fuses, either damp, missing or broken that needed him to fiddle with, buy or fix. Finally, we would be ready and then the starter motor either clicked pathetically and wouldn't start or the engine would roar into life with shocking power and I would have to race down off the roof to push the gear stick to neutral, as Dad was at the stern.

I should mention here that I was perforce

my father's boat-boy. He didn't have a son, I was four years older than the next sister down, so I was it. Mother had no intention of messing about with oily stuff or trying to do things with engines. Her job was to organise the food. Her idea of boating was that somebody else did it and her idea of swimming was inspired by those old films, where glamorous women in bathing caps covered with flowers swam languid side-stroke in lagoons.

Sometimes Dad had to go and buy a new anchor. Thea was a small boat but prone to anchor loss. This was because we dropped anchor somewhat randomly, either in very sandy areas where they would drag with the current and prevailing wind or else, worse, in very rocky areas, where they would frequently get wedged as the boat moved around. I would stand at the prow with the anchor while Dad pondered, then he would shout, "Righto, throw it in!"

Whereupon I would splosh the steel anchor into the sea as Dad backed up to pull it tight. I would then pull the rope to see if the anchor was holding – sometimes it was and sometimes it wasn't, which would mean doing it again. Sometimes it seemed to be at first and we would all be eating our picnic when we would notice the boat had drifted too close to rocky land and we'd have to haul up the anchor and push her out a bit again. The dogs would, by this time, be hot and need to cock their legs, so Mother in a hat and little sister, Sally, would disembark into Dora with dogs and Dad would row them to shore, while Trudi and I swam together to the beach.

Eventually, the time would come for us to leave. How exciting! What would the anchor do? There were three options:

a) it would come up like a dream as I pulled it

b) Dad would go back and forth over it while I pulled and after a while it would come free

or

c) it was stuck.

If it was c) I would have to dive in, follow the rope ten or twelve feet or so down to the anchor and heave it about a bit to try and free it. I would do this a few times and sometimes there was a jubilant moment of success but if not, I took a Stanley knife down with me to saw through the rope if I couldn't undo the knot. Dear Father couldn't open his eyes in the sea or indeed even swim down to the anchor. He wasn't keen on putting his head underwater. But there we are, there would be another Miller anchor in Davy Jones's Locker[20], and we would chug our way back without it.

One Sunday we went off down to Aberdeen Harbour, all set for a lovely day. We noticed it was strangely crowded. Every single space along every dock was occupied, the mighty junks were bedecked with flags and lots of sampans were drifting about with people standing on board. I didn't think anything of it, except that we would have to navigate ourselves carefully through the throng and I flung myself onto the lilo on the top of the boat, tucked my little radio under my ear and settled down in peace while Dad did whatever he did. After a time I heard him say to Mum, "Well, I don't know what's the matter with this thing, Thel."

Oh no I thought, don't involve me...! Then I suppose he noticed the crowds. I opened an eye to watch him as he squeezed the hooter to test it and then he said mildly, "Now that's a bit of a nuisance, the hooter's stopped working, too."

The problem was, Dad explained, the gears kept jamming and would only operate in third gear or neutral. Dad demonstrated this to us but nothing he tried seemed to get the engine into first gear. Ah well, thought our parents, we will just have to manage as it is. It didn't ever occur to them to give up and go home.

"Mary, you go in front with the boat hook and if we get too near anyone just push off," said Dad as he started the engine. Obediently, I stood in the prow like a young teenage figurehead in my pink denim shorts and frilly bikini top, the long boat hook held like a lance at the ready. Off we went in third gear at a rate of knots, weaving in and out of all the floating traffic, with me standing, Valkyrie-like, wielding the boat hook and shouting, "Beep beep! Beep beep!" by way of a warning. Sampans scattered and grandmothers, dogs and children stared down at us from the huge junks as we sped on our way, until we hit the main channel, when I heard Dad shout to me, "Keep your eyes open darling, I can't seem to stop it." Thea, it seemed, was temporarily (we hoped) unstoppable.

That was when we discovered why there were so many boats and people about. We zoomed into the central channel as eight dragon boats raced towards us, the rowers straining and sweating, my increasingly hoarse *beeps* unheard as they bore down upon us. The crowds on the various spectating boats screamed and shouted. Vast sums of betting money were involved, people's fortunes were made or lost at such an event and Thea was about to mess up the race.

"Oh blast," Dad said, managing somehow accidentally to get the engine into fourth. We sped along at a rate of knots in front of the racers. A police boat suddenly appeared and the officer yelled, "Jow-la!" (Get Out!"). Dad shouted back something polite and waved cheerily as we whizzed past them.

"Stop!" cried the officer.

"We can't," I shouted back, but then I heard Dad telling me to say nothing and so on we went in front of the racing dragon boats, speeding away from the rowers and first to cross the finishing line as we headed full pelt out to sea.

Dad's face was wreathed in smiles. "Well, that was fun!" he said.

Here's Dad in his Auxiliary Marine Police uniform.
He's first right after the big guy with the ring.

Apart from being beautiful and having various other attributes, Mother was an excellent dancer. Her indolent, side-stroke swimming style belied her sporty nature; she had once won the Hong Kong Ladies Tennis Championships after all! But her real love was ballroom dancing. Before we upped sticks and left for Hong Kong, she and her brother-in-law had done well in county dancing championships. I can imagine Dad and his sister, Brenda, sitting at a table at the side of the dance floor, he nursing half a pint of warm bitter, she with her whisky mac, while glumly watching their spouses spinning around the floor in a whirlwind of taffeta and tails.

My father, for all his musical abilities, was not good at dancing. He danced – I use the word loosely – with his body held stiffly upright, not for him the graceful swoop and bend, the swift-footed tripping of the light fantastic, the elegant dip of the head towards his swooning partner... oh no! Rigidly, he did the two-step with metronomic precision and no style.

One day Mother decided she'd had enough. He would have to learn. No longer could he get away with explaining plaintively that boys' schools in the 1930s were not hotbeds of dancing prowess, or that none of his masters had ever suggested he quickstep down the hallowed school corridors or waltz around the school hall after double maths. She would take no more excuses, she said firmly. So, she looked around for a dancing teacher. It was then that she came across Nip's Dancing School in Wan Chai.

"Harold," she announced one day, "I've booked a session at Nip's Dancing School. It will be lovely."

"Nip's Dancing School? Nip along to Nips?" he answered facetiously.

Mum rolled her eyes. "But will you come?"

"Of course my darling," said Dad, as he always did.

So it was that our parents went off to dance at Nip's, to the delight of Mother and the resignation of Father. Apparently, the Nips had run a similar, but much posher, school of dance in Shanghai before coming as refugees to Hong Kong. Here, they had rented a rickety dance hall one floor up an uneven staircase, somewhere in the dark side streets of Wan Chai and this dubious venue had become their reborn dancing school.

It was an exciting challenge, Mother said, just getting up the steep, crooked stairs in her stiletto heels, but it was worth it, for once you opened the door of the school a scene of such lushness and glamour met their eyes that they were mesmerised. The Nips had spared no corner of the room or ceiling from their decorative efforts – silver and gold hangings, chandeliers, tiny white velvet-covered chairs, multiple mirrors and fairy lights festooned every inch.

In the midst of all this glittering glory stood Mr and Mrs Nip. Mrs Nip resplendent in floor length evening gown and elbow length gloves, her black hair piled on her head and embedded with crystal jewels, and Mr Nip, equally arresting in white tie and tails, his hair gleamingly Brylcreemed, his shoes polished to a mirror shine and flaunting two inch elevator heels.

The second thing our parents noticed after recovering from the effects of the décor, was the miniature size of the Nips. Mrs Nip was just about five feet tall and Mr Nip, a couple of inches taller. My parents were not huge by any means, Mum being five-and-a-half feet and Dad, five feet ten inches. However, any concern they had about how awkward it might be to dance with these tiny people was resolved quickly. After the introductions, and once they had started the music, Mr Nip swept Mother into his arms authoritatively and with a beautific smile upon his face - which lined up perfectly with Mother's delightful cleavage - they immediately set off around the room, the circling mirrored lights above them reflecting their seamless progress.

Mrs Nip turned to Dad with a smile, I

suppose assuming that since Mum danced so well, her husband surely would, too. She soon discovered the ghastly truth. After a momentary hesitation, she gathered herself together and grasped him with her tiny, strong hands. With fierce determination she pushed him around the room, while he remained as inflexible as a plank. Her expostulations rose above the music. "Mr Mirra! No! Not that way! I tell you when you do that! Now you do like this..!" She pulled and pummelled him into compliance. Her tiny feet in their crushed velvet, sequinned stilettos kept nudging his ankles, their sharp heels perilously close to his toes. And all the while, oblivious to their struggles Mr Nip and Mother, blissfully smiling in a dream of perfectly coordinated footsteps, bounced and whizzed past them dancing the American Smooth.

Dad was less than enthusiastic about going back to Nip's Dancing School for the second and any subsequent time given the further mortification he expected to endure at the hands of Mrs Nip. But Mother was so pleased and looked forward to it so much he offered himself up in the spirit of the sacrificial lamb.

However, Mrs Nip was not a woman to be defeated. Like most Chinese women she was implacably determined. He had come to learn to dance something and so learn to dance something he would. She would bend Dad, literally and figuratively, to her iron will. He liked to step in time? Then the cha-cha-cha it would be! One, two – one, two, three, one, two - etc. This, Father found he could do! She choreographed the perfect dance for Dad, with a set variation on the cha-cha-cha theme. Forwards, back, cha-cha-cha, back, forwards, cha-cha-cha, then cross to the right, cha-cha-cha cross to the left... and repeat. She even introduced a little twirl or two eventually, much to her satisfaction. Dad came home full of the joys of spring and taught it all to me; I became his cha-cha-cha practice partner and in fact the last time we danced the cha-cha-cha together was the Christmas before he died, he was ninety at the time.

Mr and Mrs Nip were very eager to expand. They dreamed that the glories of their Shanghai Dancing School of yesteryear might once again be theirs in Hong Kong, after all the troubles and difficulties they had faced, and Mother was pleased to help. During the winter months our church held popular Scottish country dancing sessions in the church hall, much loved by all, especially the many Scots in the congregation and not least my parents (even Dad, since you were either walking or skipping in an unwavering pattern). Mum thought the Scottish dancers might be a likely source of clients for the Nips. She drew a large flyer up for the church notice board:

Enjoy Dancing?
Come to the
FAMOUS
NIP'S SCHOOL OF DANCE
Shanghai! Hong Kong! London and Paris!

embellished with cut-out pictures from magazines of gorgeous, glamorous film stars in dancing mode such as Marilyn Monroe, Ginger Rogers and Princess Grace, with the school address at the bottom.

This turned out to be a gold mine. The Nips didn't know what had hit them; large, kilted men and red-haired ladies of solid girth made their jolly way up the rickety staircase, to bend and strut to the Argentine tango. The eldest of the Nip's sons was dragooned into the family business although only about sixteen then, a much taller version of Mrs Nip, including the long hair and determination.

Soon a licensee set up a tiny, black leather bar in a corner of the room for interval drinks. Then the restaurant downstairs astutely arranged to send a dinner-suited waiter up with cocktail snacks half way through the evening. And everyone was happy! Everyone was making money! It was boom time Chez Nip! Mr Nip bought Mother a gift of Chanel No 5 and Dad some fancy whisky for Christmas, completely unexpectedly but of course very happily received.

I have often wondered if Nip's Dancing School is still there$_{21}$; perhaps a third generation of Nips is gliding over the parquet flooring even as I write? Or, possibly at Nip's Ecole de Danse in Paris? Or at NIPZ, Kensington, London W1? That would be nice.

LANTAU ISLAND, HONG KONG, 1960

For a couple of years, when we were young teenagers, my school friend Janet and I went to the island of Lantau to spend a fortnight with her father. We would catch the ferry from Queen's Pier$_{22}$ and bob across the sea, leaving the raucous noise of Hong Kong behind for the large, peaceful and pastoral haven that was Lantau island in those days, with very few tarmac roads and very few people.

Janet's dad was a government waterworks engineer at the time, and he and his men were building an enormous reservoir to augment the supplies to Hong Kong in the summer. So many people had fled to Hong Kong from China that Hong Kong's own reservoir reserves were inadequate and for several summers we had only four hour's water supply every four days, most of which the Hong Kong Government had to buy from China. It was an uneasy arrangement and depended uncomfortably on the whims of Mao's government. Furthermore, people were getting fed up with collecting water from standpipes at six o'clock in the morning and with China threatening not to supply us at all, annoyingly frequently.

So, Janet's dad and his team were busy on Lantau island, building locks, dams, walls and other mighty things involving diggers and huge holes and enormous pipes, none of whose functions I can either recall or understand, now or then. I do remember staring blankly at it all from the top of a huge bank of earth, dressed in an adored pair of denim shorts and a tee shirt and longing to get back to the beach, while Janet's dad stood stockily in his long white shorts and open neck shirt explaining things to us. He had a thick streaky shock of blond hair, a tanned face and bright blue eyes, and spoke with a strong Scottish accent. We would dutifully stand there listening to him, for we both admired and respected him. He was kind and fair but quite authoritarian so that as young teenagers we felt free to dream and listen to our music, living safely and easily within his parameters.

It was the beach and the sea that Janet and I loved. We would lean our arms across the wide, cool, stone windowsill of our bedroom in Janet's dad's house, the big steel ceiling fan whirring unnoticed above our heads, and gaze down the rocky path through the pines to the sea. The green, tree-clad land curved round in a great arc as if it were capturing the blue-green water in the arms of its silvery beach, five miles long, empty, beckoning and blisteringly hot. We would spend our afternoons lying on the white sand in a soporific daze beside our abandoned homework, idling the time away as teenage girls do, speculating on various boys at school and bursting into vacuous giggles over nothing. We spent hours lolling around in the sea, as brown as berries, as fit as any young and free creatures and in a way, waiting for our lives to begin.

Sometimes Janet's dad would tell us to put on our glad rags as he was going to take us with him to the little town of Silvermine Bay. We rushed about dressing ourselves up and then jumped into the back of his rough and seatless old Land Rover. We stood there clinging to the overhead railings as he lurched and swayed at speed down the uneven track to the town, through the peppery scented pines, the buzzing cicadas, the sun going down over the sea to the right, the mountains to the left, us laughing and shrieking and he occasionally shouting "hang on girls!" The evening drew in, the air was soft and scented. The lethargy of the day left us and high spirits overtook us all.

Eventually, we would draw in to Silvermine Bay, then something resembling a three-horse town in the Wild West. I can't imagine how it is now. A few little streets, a few shops, a rough wooden bridge over the stream, a few open-air restaurants serving wonderful Chinese food al fresco, and a few bars. One of these was fondly known as The Club by the waterworks men. There was a jukebox, which Janet's dad gave us a few coins to play on while he drank beer, played darts or cards and horsed around. He would buy us some crisps and a Green Spot orangeade each and we watched and listened to the men. At weekends some highly blonde and brown-tanned women would sometimes appear. They laughed and smoked and we listened to the increasingly bawdy larking about between the men and women, until finally he decided that was enough, would round us up and home we would go in the Land Rover.

This was the very best part of the evening and why I wanted to come with him so much. Janet's dad drove home very slowly along the track, sometimes singing quietly, mostly not. The stars were dense in the night sky, as if they were so close and bright they were in danger of falling on to us. The incessant *zizz zizz zizz* of the cicadas accompanied us as we stood in the back of the vehicle, holding onto the poles at the side and gazing up at the magnificent night sky. The Land Rover swayed slowly along the track and we heard his nice baritone voice intermittently but we girls were silent, sniffing the pine-scented air and breathing the smell of the sea. There were no lights, no cars. Janet's dad, after a few beers, drove gently along. Tears came to my eyes at the beauty of the night. Spending two weeks doing little with Janet was worth it, just for this. Even now I can cast myself back to those times. Her dad at the wheel in a rather sweat-stained pink shirt, Janet and I leaning together as we hung on to the rails of the Land Rover swinging slowly down the track, with the sound of *You Take the High Road* hummed under his breath.

The bungalow Janet's dad lived in was stark, in the way a man's house is without a woman. No rugs graced the stone floor, no flowers on the table, and no curtains at the windows. Her mum allegedly hated Lantau. It was, she said, too hot, too full of insects, too boring and too remote. And there were snakes. That was true. This suited all of us very well; she stayed in a semi-constant state of high dudgeon in their air-conditioned flat in Hong Kong and we enjoyed the peace and calm without her. Fortunately, our needs were in fact catered for, because the government had provided an amah to cook and clean and she it was who would be waiting for us as we drove up from our evening out. She would meet us with a beaming smile on her face, her long black pigtail down her back bobbing as she greeted us, dressed as was usual in those days in a white Chinese side-buttoned top and loose black trousers. She would bring us drinks and peanuts, a San Miguel beer for Janet's dad and two Green Spots for us. The three of us would sit on the verandah with our feet up on the railing, gazing at the sea and stars, cogitating the meaning of life, while I covertly glanced at the golden hairs on Janet's dad's brown legs, glinting in the light of the moon.

Sadly, as all idylls must, these periods of

peaceful delight would come to an inevitable end. We girls would slump morosely on the wooden benches of the ferry back to Hong Kong, surrounded by our various tatty bags of belongings, as it pulled away from Lantau pier and chugged out to sea. Slowly, the great green island of Lantau slipped away from us, as we glumly watched the tiny moving dot that was Janet's dad's Land Rover weaving its way along the slash of red that was the track along the base of the mountain, he going his way and we going ours.

Farewell, farewell, peace of mind and heart.

THE GREAT TAO

Mother had a propensity for gathering bizarre acquaintances. Should I call them friends? Possibly, I could, though they were actually people with various peculiarities, who recognised a kind and interested woman, who would listen without judgement. To allow such a man over her doorstep, for a start, and then to sit with him and give him tea, well, it would have been an incomprehensible act for a Chinese lady sixty years ago.

That is why a young man called Peter Ho came to the door of our particular mansion flat in Hong Kong, knowing we were Europeans, initially to sell encyclopedias. Mum invited him in, probably because she had a few spare minutes and he looked so keen and earnest, with his little pale face behind his large tortoiseshell glasses. She thought it would be harsh not to let him give her the sales patter he had obviously spent many hours learning.

However, his utter lack of a sense of humour coupled with his Cantonese idiosyncrasies, one of which was to use random, or no articles or prepositions to speak of, made his words sound much more lecture than conversation. On this particular day he informed her firmly and at length how much she needed his offering, not to mention just how wrong she would be to deny her children the Encyclopedia Britannica and thus ruin their entire future lives. The word *wrong* figured highly in Peter's monologues.

Mum was quite accustomed to being lectured to, not least by me. I was fourteen and felt I knew a great deal more about everything than she did, so when he eventually came to a halt, unperturbed, she asked him if he would like some tea, seeing as how he had been talking for some considerable time. Then she made the mistake of asking him kindly how he came to be selling the Encyclopedia, whereupon he launched into a long and melodramatic account of his woebegone life. Suffice it to say, though Mother did not buy the Encyclopedia, she did acquire Peter Ho.

There followed, over the years, many visits from Peter. Having abandoned the Britannica, his next excursion into door-to-door selling was insurance, whereupon he lectured Mother about how *wrong* it would be for her to deny her children the money they would receive through his product when she died - as die she must since she was now getting old... She blinked her large blue eyes at him, somewhat taken aback since she was then thirty-seven and constantly being told how beautiful she was. Typical Peter. A man with as much empathy as a brick.

Sometimes he dropped in unannounced when he felt the urge to deliver his views on any particular subject. He would ring the bell, one of us would open the door, look at Mum, roll our eyes and disappear immediately. From our various rooms we could hear him droning on about who knew what, just grateful to have escaped because Mum was quite capable of corralling us to share the pain. No thanks!

Mother was a wonderful mimic. Our family dinners every night could last for hours since there were often five girls and Mum and Dad, all anxious to talk. Dad finally tried to impose a scheme where each of us would have five uninterrupted minutes, and when it was her turn Mum would mimic Peter hilariously: "Mrs Mirra, you must try harder, understand how necessary to give children good education!" he pontificated through her, wagging his finger, "they must work harder! They must study to be successful! I have many books on this subject! I will bring many to you!"

Mum as Peter, would lean back in her chair, nodding vigorously, then she would add, "not very expensive!"

At one time he had flirted with becoming a Catholic and she heard all about how wrong it would be of her not to save her children's souls by becoming Catholic too, but Mum actually drew the line under that. So he unconverted because he did, over time, learn to listen to Mum once he had run out of steam.

One day Mum told Dad and me in no uncertain terms that we were to stay in the sitting room with her the following afternoon and not skive off because Peter had arranged to come and inform her about how she should live her life embracing his latest passion – Taoism[23]. Neither Dad nor I was enthusiastic as we both felt Mum had made her bed and it was she who would have to lie on it, but she cajoled us until we could withstand her no longer. So, the following day we put out the teacups on the coffee table and awaited our fate.

Although it was a scorching day, Peter arrived with a white tasselled Taoist scarf draped ostentatiously over the shoulders of the dark suit he always wore for his visits to Mum. I'm not sure he was any more delighted to see Dad and me than we were to see him, since his whole reason for coming was to spend as much time as possible brow-beating Mother. He shook hands and we sat down. Mum poured the tea and then Peter started:

"Mrs Mirra, you must try very hard understand concept of Oneness."

Mum blinked, "Oh yes?" she said.

"The whole world is One," declared Peter, "I am also me and I am also One! And you also are one with me! And also Mr Mirra - and Miss Mirra too, is also One," he added disparagingly; he would probably have liked to have excluded us.

Dad took a gulp of tea. "Would you like a biscuit, Peter?" he asked.

"Biscuit? Oneness of world is important, Mr Mirra!"

"Certainly it is, indeed," replied Dad.

"Oneness is meaning of life, not biscuit!" he frowned crossly at Dad.

I tried not to laugh. Mum was going a bit pink. "Err, Peter, please tell us, how do we attain Oneness?" she enquired soothingly.

"I'll go and get some shortbread anyway," I offered, not sure I could keep a straight face.

"Thank you dear," replied Mum.

"I'll help you," added Dad swiftly. We scarpered off to the kitchen and tried not to laugh while we put shortbread and digestives onto two plates so it didn't look too silly that we had gone off together. We returned to Peter's stentorious tones.

"Mrs Mirra, I have some pamphlets for you." He waved a collection of luridly coloured leaflets under her nose, then nearly knocked his tea over them as he put them down with a flourish on the coffee table. A large, single eye stared coldly up at us under the heading The Center For Oneness: Life and the Great Tao.

"We must study to understand the mystery of the Big Toe, Mrs Mirra."

"Ah yes. Mmm," said Mum.

"The Big Toe sees all things," announced Peter, helping himself to shortbread, "It is complete knowledge that you must attain. Everything in world is explained by Big Toe."

"I'll just go and put the kettle on for more tea," I said helplessly, longing to get back to the kitchen before hysteria overtook me. Dad followed, bringing an empty plate, ostensibly to replenish all the biscuits that Peter had eaten his way through. Once we had shut the kitchen door we clutched each other, shaking with suppressed laughter as Dad wiggled his knobbly big toe in his flipflops at me.

Mother flung open the door. "Are you two coming with more tea and biscuits?" she demanded, mouthing recriminations at us and beckoning us to follow her back to where Peter waited impatiently, his flow interrupted.

"I am so sorry Peter, they had to find another packet of shortbread," we heard her lie as we returned.

"I want you read pamphlets to learn most important aspect of Oneness of Big Toe that give you improvement in your life, Mr Mirra," Peter said sternly to Dad, who nodded thoughtfully. He glanced at me, about to explode with my barely controlled giggles.

"Certainly," Dad said, "I look forward to attaining oneness with my Big Toe. But as you said earlier Peter, education is most important and Mary has to do her homework now, so we will have to say goodbye."

Both Mum and Peter gave him an icy glare,

for much the same reason. Dad and I walked down the hallway to my room, and once inside collapsed on the bed in hysterics. Laughter suppressed is so impossible not to give in to! For decades we only had to intone, "The Big Toe" to each other and we would be giggling again.

Happy Days. Peter gave up Taoism having made no converts, and took up selling electrical goods instead. Thus it was that Mum presented Dad with an electric carving knife for Christmas, which he ignored, continuing to use Grandad's ultra sharp, steel knife as he always had.

Unexpectedly, I found the electric knife, untouched and still in its box, when I cleared out my parents' bungalow after their deaths.

TYPHOON

Typhoon Squatter huts on Hong Kong island.

I woke suddenly, to find Mother standing beside my bed, fully dressed. It was one o'clock in the morning.

"Come on, wake up!' she demanded.

"What's the matter?"

"I just can't believe it! Can't you hear it? How can you be asleep?"

I was, after all, a Hong Kong girl, a girl who could sleep through two separate pile drivers *ker-plunk, ker-plunking* their way through the granite to build another high rise. Or through the high pitched squealing, accompanied by the dramatic clash of cymbals, of the Chinese opera much beloved of Ah Oi, coming from the back wash room as she scrubbed her way through the washing.

However, I now realised there was a noise like a thousand banshees crashing around outside, shaking the windows, howling down the chimneys and whistling deafeningly through the cracks and loose fittings of the old, metal window frames. In my shortie pyjamas I went into the sitting room where Dad and Ah Chun were sticking wide strips of tape in stars across all the windows – this was a vital exercise to prevent, as much as it is possible to prevent, the windows blowing in. Once they do that, you have to abandon the room and cower elsewhere until the typhoon$_{24}$ blows itself out. This isn't just because the wind blows in rain, but also because the mad, violent, unpredictable wind can pull you out of the room if you are too near a broken window, or blow in a large object, which could hit you on the head and potentially knock you out.

I should have been better prepared for this marathon night. We had all been sent home from school at lunchtime because of the typhoon warnings. When we'd left home in the morning the typhoon warning was signal number one, which meant we had to go to school. By midday it had gone up to signal number three with number five imminent, so school was closed and those of us from Hong Kong side had jubilantly packed up our stuff and leapt with alacrity onto the bus to the Star Ferry.

The sea was choppy and we were all in high spirits, clambering up the unsteady wooden gangway onto the ferry as it bumped and groaned against the concrete pier. Rain was pouring down and sloshing across the decks, and the sea splashed over us as we huddled together excitedly. The ferry chugged and bounced across the harbour as number five signal was hoisted, which meant we had in fact caught the last ferry across to Hong Kong as the ferry stopped running after that.

A battered junk in the harbour after a typhoon.

Through the rain we could see the boats, large

and small, the wallah-wallahs$_{25}$, the sampans and the ocean-going junks, rushing helter skelter as fast as they could into the safety of the typhoon shelters. It was a wonderful sight in a way, everything going full pelt to get to safety; the massive junks with their full sails being furled as they relied on their engines now that they had arrived in the harbour. The sampans bobbed about from crest to crest across the waves.

We hurried off the ferry once we had reached Hong Kong side. None of us ever worried about being wet, there was no escape from the rain in a typhoon, and we half ran through the town and up Garden Road to the Peak Tram terminus, carrying our shoes since rainwater was swishing down the hill ankle deep, very anxious to get there before the tram stopped, too. We were lucky.

When we got home, things seemed to be a little quieter. With a typhoon you simply couldn't tell which way it was going to veer, and during the afternoon we had a few hours when it looked as if it was going to head off back to the Philippines. Goodbye being off school we sighed, half sorry and half glad she was going.

We had an uneventful supper and went to bed, but sometime after midnight the typhoon returned with a vengeance. The wind was screaming around our building and although we were three floors up, branches and even whole trees were blowing past at amazing speeds. Soon all of us were frantically rolling up Mum's precious rugs to lift them off the floor on to tables and chairs, moving everything into the middle of rooms and most important of all, once the windows had been taped, going on towel duty.

It was 1962 and we'd had quite a bit of experience of major typhoons, particularly around two years earlier when Typhoon Mary[26] had hit Hong Kong with vicious ferocity, so I remembered with a degree of loathing, towel duty. It was the most tiring and tedious job that you had to tackle during a typhoon, if you lived in an old building with ill-fitting windows. You had to roll towels up loosely, put them on the floor under the windows to catch the rain which the typhoon was blowing in at speeds of sometimes 150mph or more at a horizontal angle, then almost immediately wring them out into a bucket when they were soaked through and start the process again. Then you had to take the buckets and empty them in the bathroom.

The worst thing about it was how unrelenting it was! Outside, it was dark and strange; the low pressure made you feel odd, and you couldn't talk because of the extreme level of noise. All you could do was try to stop the house being flooded. We were fortunate enough to live in a solid block of flats built in 1910, which had withstood the Japanese during the war so I didn't fear for my life - which was a benefit not shared by the refugees, exposed to the elements in their inadequate hillside shacks.

Gradually, the darkness of the night grew lighter and dawn broke. Outside, we could now see the devastation this typhoon had brought and was still bringing after six hours of total havoc. The road was covered with uprooted trees and branches; cars had been blown sideways or turned over. There was of course nobody about. Still, she (they were all *she* in those days) blew on, although by now she had dropped from typhoon signal ten to five. We were all so weary.

Later, we discovered Typhoon Wanda was one of the worst typhoons in history and nearly five hundred people had died, mainly those poor people living in the temporary refugee shacks, which were thrown together out of sheets of tin and cardboard, perched on the edges of Kowloon's mountains. As fast as the Hong Kong Government could build resettlement blocks to house them, new refugees escaped from the Red Guards in Mao's China, arriving with nothing but the clothes on their backs. The government's aim was to house immigrants within two years of their arrival but in the interim they had to live how they could, although medicine and schooling was available, and free, immediately.

Fortunately, Dad had parked his car around the back in the garage for once, so it was unharmed. The typhoon reduced to a tropical storm before heading away from China, only to build up again to wreak destruction back in the Philippines. For us, though, she was gone and an unholy quiet descended.

In the late afternoon we got in the car and drove down town to see what had happened. Landslides and fallen trees half blocked the road down the Peak and lumps of broken bricks and concrete, which had blown off buildings, lay scattered about. It was strangely silent, no birds sang and it was drizzling with rain.

Once we reached town, however, the real damage could been seen and it was bizarre – huge cargo ships that had been anchored in the harbour had been blown inland and lay haphazardly on the street, not just on the first road along the coast but even the second. Cars were sideways and upside down. All the protective plastic sheeting and green netting that had been draped round buildings while construction was going on now blew around on the ground, and most of the bamboo scaffolding had also been pulled off the buildings and was lying in pieces on roofs and pavements. No trams could run; the tram tracks were covered in detritus.

We stared at all this devastation in awe and horror. Then we went home to empty the dehumidifiers that were rumbling away constantly, and to try and dry out our flat.

NANCY

My parents had a close friend called Nancy. I thought the world of her; she was a bit younger than most of their friends, and she had an extremely youthful outlook on the world. Her background was interesting, not least because like my *Auntie* Mary she also came from Shanghai, but their circumstances could not have been more different. I've always thought how strange it is that people can end up in the same place in the same country at the same time through such dissimilar and circuitous routes...

Nancy started life in some dirt poor rural village somewhere near Shanghai. Being a girl she had very little value in those days, when poor parents would frequently put their baby daughters outside in the cold to die. She was born, I believe, around 1931 or 1932. Whether her parents cared about her or not, they decided they couldn't afford to keep her and besides they needed money to feed their sons. So they sold her.

The relatively wealthy man who bought her had a family of his own. It was not uncommon for a girl to be brought into a family as a servant or I suppose you could say, a slave. She would be brought up as both companion and domestic worker until puberty and then probably become a concubine. This was Nancy's projected life pattern. However, she happened to be extremely beautiful, with wide eyes and fair skin, and her owner had connections at that time with a number of Shanghai filmmakers. Nancy by then, roughly fourteen I suppose, had grown into a very attractive, although very young woman, something that became noticed by one of her owner's older film producer friends.

By exactly what route Nancy was either gifted or sold to this elderly film producer and for what bargain or remuneration I don't know, but this beautiful girl was from that point on a film ingénue, on the arm of what I can only surmise was an unattractive and relatively old man. She then became pregnant and had a baby, who it seems she was able to look after adequately since the old man didn't seem to resent the child and provided an amah to care for the boy, while Nancy was being paraded around as his companion.

At this point Nancy was about sixteen or seventeen, and her life took another unexpected turn; she was taken to a gathering where there were some foreign guests. She was obviously very pretty and so was quickly noticed by these European men. However, they were well aware that she was the companion of the filmmaker and were therefore fairly circumspect. Nancy either didn't explain to me, or she did but I have forgotten, what happened and how she came to meet and was able to interact with the foreigners, but I assume she had learned some English during her time as a minor film star so probably it was possible for her to talk to them a little, given the opportunity.

There was a young man within this group called Thomas, who found himself becoming very attracted to Nancy. When he discovered she was not just a free film starlet but was actually owned by the old man, he was appalled. They grew close. Nancy found herself falling in love for the first time, but didn't think it was possible for her to have a loving future given that she had a little son. Thomas didn't give up though and hatched a plan of escape, having promised always to care for both her and her child. One night they did escape and somehow made their way down to Hong Kong. It must have been difficult and dangerous and I admire their bravery!

Thomas was as good as his word. He treated her son as his own once they had safely reached Hong Kong. As Nancy had never been formally adopted, employed, indentured or married, had no birth certificate nor even a known birth date, she in fact had no status at all until she reached Hong Kong and came under the regulated norms of the British Crown colony.

There had always been a trickle, and later

a flood, of people fleeing life in China and coming into Hong Kong. Many of them had questionable antecedents, or no paperwork, or the paperwork they did have was confused or incomprehensible, so the authorities were realistic about the situation in which people found themselves. Hong Kong's government operated on a laissez-faire principle in this regard.

Nancy told them she thought she was eighteen, which was adequate for the authorities to accept her as an adult. Furthermore, she spoke Shanghainese$_{27}$ as her mother tongue so they were able to record her birthplace as being Shanghai. She did have a few photographs of herself from various magazines dressed as a glamorous film starlet, which she showed Mum and me once, but whether she ever allowed anyone in authority to see them is doubtful. I assume she wouldn't have wanted many people to know who or where she was.

I believe the film producer made efforts to catch her and bring her back, but of course he had no right to do so from the legal point of view once she was registered in Hong Kong - he had no legal rights over her at all since he had never acknowledged the child or his mother. So, she and Thomas married and Thomas adopted Nancy's little son and some time later they went on to have a daughter of their own.

By the time we met them they were a

well established couple and I liked and admired Nancy no end, not particularly for her bravery or her background since these aspects of her life I knew very little about at that age, but because she was so light-hearted, glamorous, funny and warm. We were much the same size when I was a young teenager, and she had such lovely clothes! She generously gave me many of them. She and Thomas and their children used to be good friends with my parents and I was always glad to see her; her pretty, sparkling eyes and her happy smile.

With regret, I have to say her life was relatively short and we were all devastated when she died but I believe she would never have wanted to live it in any other way.

CHURCH AND WALKS, SNAKES
AND HAPLESS YOUTHS

On Sunday mornings our family went to church. This was not as straightforward as it sounds – it took planning, vision, effort and perseverance to get us all ready to go. Presumably the age and gender of those needing to be rounded up contributed to the challenge. There were three daughters and sometimes two other girls staying with us at our flat and all had to be woken, breakfasted, showered, dressed, coiffed and mollified prior to embarkation, and all this by ten o'clock in the morning. Looking back now, this seems a daunting task but somehow it happened, week after week. Father would wander around, saying, "Come along girls, it's getting late," randomly, while everyone argued over who was wearing what and which dress looked best and who had nicked whose clothes.

Dad would eventually sit on the piano stool and watch despairingly as young ladies ebbed and flowed between bedrooms. Sometimes I sat beside him. The stool faced the various bedroom doors so the action was fast and furious.

"If they had only told me," he sighed.

"Told you what?"

"When I was a boy in the army, that I'd be sitting here twenty years later, watching a plethora of nymphs like this."

"Shame there's no shepherds to take them away," I said darkly. "They drive me crazy."

Dad played the tune, *Nymphs and Shepherds, Come Away* and we sang a few bars, until we were interrupted by, "Ouch, ouch, ouch!" from a bedroom where Mother, without the slightest compassion, was dragging the hairbrush through my youngest sister Sally's long hair as she shrank piteously away. You could hear the clatter of the myriad golden charms on Mother's bracelet as she relentlessly pulled out the knots. A timpani of charms.

Dad suddenly looked at me, "I assume you, at least, are ready?"

I looked down at my bare feet, jumped up and ran off to find some shoes.

We had progressed to the penultimate step – Dad playing Mendelssohn's sonorous *Pilgrims' March* with the loud pedal on to hurry us up. The action had picked up, the girls had put another layer on over their underwear and were now fighting about shoes. Mother had snaffled Trudi and pulled the socks out of her starter bra. Sally had neat plaits. I had found my handbag.

Down the stairs we went, and into the ghastly, overwhelming smell of the hot leather seats in the car, mixed with Mother's Worth Je Reviens perfume. There was, of course, considerable forceful discussion about whose turn it was to sit by the windows. I am glad to say that being four years older than the rest of them, I generally managed to grab a window seat - unless Mother happened to intervene in the pursuit of justice as she liked to see it, rather than need, as I did.

We were all quite happy to go to church. It was (and is) a low church, simple and straightforward. We were very integrated into the church and all its doings - Father being the organist and choirmaster and Mother singing in the choir. All the younger children sat cross-legged in the front of the church for the first fifteen minutes as the first part of the service was dedicated to them. The packed congregation sang suitably cheerful, child-friendly hymns like *All Creatures Great and Small* and then the children filed out to Sunday School before the sermon began. At the end of the service, I always ran down the aisle to the organ to lean on it and Dad pulled out all the stops and played something deep and dramatic. It was thrilling to feel the power of the bass notes shuddering through us. It delighted us both.

Afterwards there was coffee in the church hall and the young drifted about, while chatting went on in the adult world, before we went home to lunch. Sometimes other people joined us but usually it was a family meal. Then afterwards, in the winter months when we didn't go out on our little boat Thea, we went for a walk.

Going for a walk doesn't sound like much of a challenge but that is only if you didn't know our parents. A walk for them was more like a trek and as we grew older, these outings became a direct test of virility and endurance for the hapless youths who became entrapped by Trudi's and my feminine wiles - or at least, smiles. We would invite them airily to join us after lunch on Sunday "for a walk with our parents and then hang out at home and play records". They did of course quite fancy that.

Setting off was a source of both pride and mortification to me because our parents had a passion for skipping. They would cross their arms behind their backs, hold hands and take off, skipping down Pokfulam Reservoir Road (a narrow path very rarely used for cars) and we would have to walk very fast, or skip ourselves, to catch up with them. The boys' eyes would boggle.

"Come on!" we'd say enthusiastically, "get a move on!" You couldn't run, it was too steep.

The truth is that unless these teenage boys got fired up about a real game such as football or hockey, they preferred to sprawl around indolently, occasionally bursting into callow laughter. Or they sat around with guitars and strummed them, also accompanied by snorts of laughter. Or sometimes they stood up to strum their guitars - or if they felt unusually energetic they threw a ball at each other. What they didn't normally do was walk a brisk five or six miles while being measured up by a girl, her parents and even her dogs.

Father would branch off the lane once skipping was over, and head into the countryside on the footpaths that ran alongside deep nullahs, which weaved all over the hillsides through the thick green vegetation. He carried his walking stick like a long conductor's baton, thwacking at the bushes from side to side as we walked along behind him.

"Does he know where he's going?" the hapless youths would whisper, the sweat on their hot faces aggravating their acne, "how long's this gonna go on?"

"Oh, I don't know," we'd reply cheerfully, "we've only just started. Why?"

Sometimes Trudi and I clambered down into the nullahs and walked along until we inevitably came to a rectangle of water. I don't know why there were built-in rectangles of water; maybe it was for any animal which had inadvertently fallen the six or seven feet into the nullah and needed a drink. However, the only animals we ever saw were snakes and that was rarely. Then we clambered up the iron rungs beside the water and walked along the path till we could climb down again. We shouted, "Snakes!" and Dad shouted, "Come out then!" and we did. This went down a treat with our young male guests.

Mother disliked snakes but she never wanted us to be scared of anything so she let our insouciance prevail. They were only the dark brown, stripy rat snakes, as thick as our arms and about a yard long, with a nasty but non-poisonous bite and a non-aggressive nature.

Less pleasant were the thin, bright green and poisonous bamboo snakes, which we mainly used to see washed into the drains by rain as we walked up to our junior school. There were also pythons in Hong Kong, but they were not interested in us as they spent most of their time coiled up asleep. They only hunted when they were hungry and as they must be one of the laziest snakes known to man they weren't hungry very often. Fortunately. When they were they didn't go after people – small barking deer or monkeys were their favourite things. On Lantau however, there were cobras.

Once we had lived for a short time in a group of high rise flats and there was a huge python living on the hillside behind them. We children used to wander around up there and a few times we saw the sleeping python curled up on a wide, flat rock and thought it was beautiful. We had no fear of it. One day there was a great hue and cry, and we rushed to look over the balcony into the car park. There, stretched out along the ground, was what we thought of as our python. The drivers and gardeners had found it and before our eyes, beheaded it. I and the other children burst into tears, gazing at the full eighteen feet of it stretched out in all its glory. Dad tried to comfort me but I wouldn't be comforted. As I remember this I still feel immensely sad about it but it meant that many people had a feast – or else they sold it and made a nice profit. Or both? Who knows?

The most dangerous snakes in Hong Kong are cobras, but they were pretty rare. Having said that, Hong Kong's famous reptile specialist Dr John Romer, whom I later interviewed several times for my radio programme on Hong Kong's snakes, died after being bitten by a king cobra on Lantau Island.

The hapless youths, however, were unaccustomed to snakes and our parents' nonchalant attitude to them - and walks and nullahs. I think we must have made their lives a misery, singing loudly as we strode along over the miles behind Dad. Our marches must have traumatised most of them.

But some it didn't – so they were invited again, poor lads.

SCHOOL DAYS

Mother had a rather casual attitude towards school. Well, education in general, I suppose. She wasn't able to matriculate herself because the Second World War started when she was sixteen and still a schoolgirl, although she was a very smart student and would have done well. So, she remained a little bitter about this for the rest of her life. At the same time, I think it demonstrated to the successful woman that she was, that school was only one facet of an education.

During the war she was what was known as a Land Girl, initially looking after horses but shortly afterwards required to kill chickens for England on a chicken farm. I could never quite get my head around her doing this as she was quite squeamish and Dad was normally called in to deal with anything nasty. But kill them she certainly did. She told me she'd decided that if she had to do it she would do it well and quickly for both her own and the chickens' sakes. She demonstrated exactly how you committed the final coup de grâce, having first chased your chicken around the yard to catch it and then having done so, swiftly wringing its neck. At that point you had to put it down and it would run around for a couple of minutes until its nerves and muscles eventually realised it was dead, so it expired.

School, to her, was somewhere I went to. It kept me out of the house and presumably taught me something until I could be released safely into the world as an adult. She did treat me as an adult in many ways as my sister Sally insists, whom I taught to read and write and to whom I read stories most nights. Being eight years older I often had to go and get her or take her somewhere, too. Recently, Sally told me she didn't remember Mum brushing her hair. She said, "You used to do it, Mary."

I don't recall when I took over this service but I suppose I did, and that was because Mother was anything but a compassionate hair brusher as I knew from bitter experience. She had Macbeth's attitude to hair brushing: "If 'twere done, when 'tis done, 'twere well 'twere done quickly."

Mother had one aim in life for her daughters - to become nice young women who had somehow managed not to get pregnant before she could dispatch us down the aisle. To that end she sent me to not just one but two different convents. She had the notion that sequestering me with a bunch of crotchety nuns would somehow create a malleable and obedient girl, not to mention that she thought if I followed the normal school progression from Peak School to King George V it might expose me to all sorts of louche boys with nefarious intentions. Suffice it to say I was very quickly expelled from both convents in quick succession and ended up at KGV anyway...

After a few weeks of my being there she relaxed and realised it was not the sink of iniquity her friends had thought, especially my Catholic Auntie Mary, and she thereby consigned her interest in my education to the dustbin. Meanwhile, Father simply wanted me to be happy. He told me once that he thought I was very bright and would do well whatever happened. I suppose that's how he had lived himself. I thrived once again with my friends, passed my exams and eventually became a prefect.

I don't remember our parents ever coming to our school - apart from once to watch a play with me in it. I was in the Sixth Form at the time. The play in question was an unlikely one for a school, called The Trojan Women, a Greek tragedy. Somehow, I became embroiled into auditioning for the Greek chorus but manoeuvred into playing the poor, benighted priestess and seer Cassandra, first raped by Ajax the Lesser and then dragged off to become the concubine of the hated conqueror, Agamemnon.

Furthermore, the person cast as my mother and also the main protagonist, Hecuba, was being acted by my friend and classmate Barbara, who was (and is of course) about five feet two inches tall, which was a bit of a joke given that I was five feet eleven inches. Not to worry, said the ever optimistic English teachers enthusiastically producing the play, "we will create a plinth in Fifth Form woodwork and Hecuba can stand on it while you do your thing around her". So, Barbara spent the entire play walking up and down this plinth about four feet from the stage floor while I acted dramatically around it.

At one point I had to rip the flowers from my hair and hurl them to the ground in despair, reciting the most dramatic speech in the entire play. The first night I managed to yank them out where they were entangled in my hair but they were white plastic and they bounced across the floor until one leapt off the stage into Mother's lap. She was sitting in the front row. Obviously, this didn't have the desired effect of conveying desperation at being dragged off by the monster Agamemnon as a concubine so in the following performances I wore real ones, equally but differently difficult to disentangle.

In true Greek tragedy style Hecuba ends up watching the burning of Troy and the deaths of her husband, children and grandchildren before being taken off as a slave to Odysseus. Barbara did a fine and suitably melodramatic job but I'm not sure as a troupe we did this play justice.

Why was this the only time I can think that our parents came to school? Talking to my sisters they pointed out that it was a long way from our house and that was true. Nevertheless, we ourselves did it five days a week. But that was then and this is now, when parents seem happy to drive their children a few hundred yards down the road, whereas we left for school before our parents were awake and our journey took around an hour and three quarters.

Ah Chun would wake me up brutally by banging open my bedroom door and shouting at me that it was "Quart to sebin" (quarter to seven) and VERY LATE and I had to get up NOW. Which I did. My sister Trudi and I would ignore the breakfast that Mother insisted was cooked for us every day. We tip-toed into our parents' room where they lay asleep - and said goodbye to them. Mum sometimes opened her eyes and said something like, "have a nice day." Then we rushed out the front door while the dogs panted with anticipation waiting for our scrambled eggs to be tipped into their bowls.

Carrying our clothing, blazers, stockings, forbidden makeup etc and our shoes if it was raining we would run to the Peak Tram and hurl ourselves through the turnstile just in time to catch the half past seven tram - often (every month) with the plaintive cry of the inspector echoing behind us: "Miss Mirra! Why you not got your season ticket yet??"

"Sorry! Sorry!" I would shout back through the windows as the tram trundled very slowly out of the station to begin its steep journey, at an angle of forty-eight degrees in parts, down the track taking us from the top of the Peak to Central.

"I'll remind my father!" I called out again as we disappeared over the edge. Dad never remembered to pay for our monthly season tickets on time. It usually took the despairing inspector two or three days to get the money out of him as he himself raced past to catch the tram, over an hour after us. Once on the tram we had about fifteen minutes to get dressed, put on the make up, brush our hair and do a bit of homework after chatting to friends and finding out the answers.

Reaching the bottom, we would hurry down Garden Road, past the Helena May and our father's office, cross over the busy main road and walk to the Star Ferry. This took us between ten and fifteen minutes, depending on the weather and our moods, but we would then arrive at the Star Ferry Concourse where Trudi and I would part company so that we could meet up with our respective friends.

Students came from all over the island to assemble at the ferry – our school was the English language high school at the time and had one thousand two hundred students of all nationalities, including quite a number of Chinese whose parents wanted them eventually to go to university in the UK, Australia or the USA. Our friends were polyglot and the image of diversity - White Russians whose families had escaped war in Russia, Russian Jews similarly who had escaped pogroms$_{28}$ and made their way to Hunan and then through China, sometimes over several generations; many Indians: Hindu, Sikh and Muslim whose families had been established traders in Hong Kong for generations, such as Lords Kadoorie$_{29}$ and Harilala and many Eurasian families who had also been there since the colony's beginning. These people, the Eurasians and others, formed the Hong Kong Defence Force battalion who fought the Japanese very bravely when they invaded the colony.

Although all lessons at school were in English and pupils enrolled to take O- and A-level examinations, it was not a typically British educational establishment. It was run on lines of its own that had developed over time. American accents or grammar, for instance, were perfectly acceptable (though not to Mother – she sent me to elocution lessons to little avail and I ended up sounding very transatlantic so that rapidly died a death). We had a structure that included prefects but which also included student consultation at every level. Field hockey and swimming were our main strengths. It educated and suited us all.

It is worth knowing the background to many of our students, born in the 1940s and 50s. During the occupation over ten thousand Commonwealth (ie. non-British) Hong Kong troops were captured by the Japanese. The Commonwealth War Graves record says this: "Treatment of such prisoners was known as being particularly harsh and cruel. Prisoners were regularly starved, beaten or tortured for even the most minor of infractions." The Japanese did not respect other races fighting for Hong Kong or Britain. Some of these people were relatives of students at school with us.

There were two Indian battalions fighting and one of them was the 5th Battalion 7th Rajput Regiment, the battalion famous for its Captain, Mateen Ansari[30], one of the bravest soldiers. In spite of the cruellest treatment because he refused to break under any and all torture or pressure, assisting his men at all times and even helping some escape the notorious Stanley Prison whilst staying behind himself, Captain Ansari was finally executed by the Japanese on October 29, 1943 in a mass beheading, alongside thirty British, Chinese and Indian soldiers under his command. He had been starved and tortured for five months before that. The Japanese wanted him to influence his Indian soldiers to work against the British. He refused. He was posthumously awarded the George Cross in 1946 for "most conspicuous gallantry" which is the highest level awarded and we were taught about him and others at school. His grave is in Stanley Military Cemetery, which I have visited. During my life in Hong Kong the Japanese were generally and vehemently hated.

So many Eurasians lost their lives fighting for Hong Kong their erstwhile considerable number was decimated, whereas they had been a notable population prior to the Japanese invasion. I had a friend, a boy whose Eurasian father, a lawyer, was not captured. He worked behind the lines, and for the whole war dressed up as a Chinese coolie and pretended to be a sweeper. He pushed a tatty cart around Stanley Village with bits of rubbish in it. Secretly, he left what food he could find by the wire netting at the camp and somehow, also secretly, soldiers would creep out of their huts at night and fetch this food, especially any eggs he could get. Cabbage or root vegetables augmented what rats they could catch and cook. People are so brave! If he had been caught not only he but his entire family would have been subjected to unimaginable suffering.

It sickens me to think that none of these Hong Kong people were accepted by China at the handover in 1997 as Hong Kong citizens because of their not being of the Han Chinese race, or because of their "contaminated" mixed ethnicity. Very few groups were as racist as those from mainland China. Then of course the children of the Portuguese families from Macau who lived and worked in Hong Kong, for instance the Remedios, Alvares and da Silva families, among others. Besides English they were Portuguese and Cantonese speaking, being ethnically mixed after the almost five hundred years (from 1557) that Portugal had its colony. Many of their members were lawyers, doctors and other professional people. And there were many children whose parents were only temporarily in Hong Kong, such as American, British and Europeans. In my last years at school the boy I was *going steady* with was Chilean-German and our close friend who made up our trio was Irish but from Trinidad. I later worked with the daughter of the Postmaster General, who was Assyrian. These were the children we knew and loved.

So, back to the ferry! Once we had all met up and done a bit of shrieking and giggling as kids do, we loaded ourselves onto the ferry and enjoyed ten minutes of bouncing around on the sea. This was the ideal time, I always thought, to finish my French homework. On Kowloon side we walked to the bus stop and caught a bus that weaved its way through the traffic of Nathan Road and into the hinterland of Kowloon, Ho Man Tin, beneath the aircraft which flew so low you could actually see the pilot in his cockpit. Finally, we got off the bus to walk the last five minutes up the road to school.

Towards the end of my school life KGV decided to employ coaches to take us to and from the ferry, which was a great innovation. It was a major hassle to catch the normal bus because

queuing was not a trait well known to the
general population, so to get onto a crowded bus
was a matter of daring, determination, energy
and sharp elbows. What a relief to step aboard a
coach!

I loved our school, KGV, with its motto,
Honeste Ante Honores[31], which I can instantly
sing if required, and I still have friends from
our schooldays over sixty years later. We were
lucky; we had a good education in all ways,
from the point of view of learning but also the
casual acceptance of our broad diversity. This
diversity meant that we dispersed to the four
corners of the globe after our A-levels. Many of
us left for Australia, as did I for a time to work
in a bookshop in Castlereagh Street, Sydney. A
lot went to America for further study and some
friends have made their home there. Others
went to university in Europe: Spain, Germany,
France and Britain. We had high quality teachers
and hard working (and playing) students. The
best of times.

Having said that, we also had some
excitingly odd teachers - but none so odd as
Mr Vaughan. Mr Vaughan was our Geography
teacher; that is, he was employed to teach us
geography and did so on and off when he felt
like it. At other times he told us stories or recited
poetry, sometimes very quietly so that you could
hear a pin drop and all of us had to gather at the
front of the geography room and crowd around

to listen to him. He was particularly fond of *The Owl and the Pussycat* by Edward Lear but was also great with *Casabianca* by Felicia Dorothea Hemans and many others, which he knew off by heart. He had a penchant for walking along the tops of the rows of long desks that we sat at. As they were not very wide and we usually had our exercise books open because we were attempting to take dictation from him, he would often stand on the pages of our books.

"Excuse me sir," we would say, "but you're standing on my book."

"Well, write around my shoe, then," was his reply and he would carry on dictating away...

Trudi and I both had shoe-shaped patterns in our Geography books. We both loved telling the assembled family at dinner of Mr Vaughan's exploits and everyone would be in fits of laughter.

He had another foible, and that was to write with chalk on the blackboard in very, very small writing. In fact, it was so small there was no chance of being able to see it without coming up to the front of the room, which we did in turn. Mr Vaughan would stand there by his desk and we had to come and copy his hieroglyphics down in groups of six, inching around him as we did.

Mr Vaughan often used his poetic Welsh voice to great effect when quoting, particularly from the Bible, which he frequently did. For instance, there was a notorious leak in the roof above the Geography room which, when it rained hard – which it did of course quite often in Hong Kong – meant the people sitting below it would get dripped on. The students who usually sat at the back of the room were the shy Chinese girls, who slunk there trying to avoid being noticed or addressed by Mr Vaughan. They were scared of not knowing how to react to his more mischievous antics, which I can perfectly understand. However, if it really rained they would have to put up their hands and point out that they were getting wet. "Sir, it's raining on us. Can we move?"

"God sends his rain upon the just and the unjust," Mr Vaughan would intone, eyes cast to heaven, and the poor girls were left to decide whether to draw attention to themselves even more by moving. Sometimes they braved it and sometimes they didn't and sat there with books or sheets of paper on their heads.

All I can say is, before the bell rang for the end of break or lunch time there would be a queue outside the Geography room waiting to be let in so we could join Mr Vaughan and enjoy the latest entertainment. And the most unlikely people actually passed Geography O-level including me, who can't tell left from right let alone have any idea of much geographically, because we all paid close attention at all times in case something exciting happened. I remember Mr Vaughan decorating the blackboard with an artwork featuring the wheat growing belt of North America and getting us to illustrate each area by drawing little pictures of wheat and horses and tractors in each place. How could you forget that?

I later found out that he had been sacked sometime after Trudi left school, when a more sober contingent of parents obviously failed to appreciate his methods.

But I daresay he had grown tired of the whole thing by then, anyway.

SUMMERTIME

Summers in Hong Kong were hot and humid. Sometimes the temperature and humidity were equal, 98 degrees Fahrenheit and 98 degrees humidity. However used to it you became it nevertheless had an effect; your beautifully straightened, fashionable hair for instance, ironed under tea towels, would turn into wet ringlets when you had hardly walked a hundred yards, with little drops of water hanging off each one, soon to drip down onto your nice, crisp white school uniform collar. Your summer uniform developed wet patches not just under your arms but down your back, where it clung to you.

Mother insisted that we had to wear shortie pyjamas or a nightie to absorb the sweat when we were sleeping because if we didn't, the sheets would be very damp in the morning and difficult to dry – nobody had driers in those days. We had a hot cupboard where there were a number of heated electric bars on all the time and the hum of the dehumidifier was a constant.

Oddly enough, because we were used to it I don't remember being upset about being drenched in sweat - when we weren't drenched with rain that is, the summer is typhoon season as well. Having to go to school so early was useful; the ferry ride was cooler and latterly we had coaches to take us to school from the Kowloon ferry pier, so all in all it wasn't too bad. The original school building was constructed for the heat; made of dark green stone with wide, covered verandahs all around to prevent direct sunlight entering the big windows of the classrooms, and grass beyond.

Our very large, grassy school field was directly in front of the building, with the cricket pavilion to the side. We were able to sit out there at lunchtime. Given the pressure on land in Hong Kong we were very lucky indeed to have such a magnificent field, a reminder of the more leisured times when the school was founded. I was absolutely useless at sport – no better at netball than tennis, running, jumping or anything at all except swimming. I spent much of the time during our frequent games periods wandering around collecting things like shuttlecocks or tennis balls from one place or another, as slowly as possible, with one or two other girls who were "off games".

One of the challenges in steamy, hot places is taking exams. We had to take our O- and A-levels at the same time as they did in England; late June and early July. We sat in the large school hall at individual desks set up in rows. The weather was very hot so we were allowed to take in blotters to lean our sweaty arms on, sweat bands to stop drips from our heads and hair onto the paper, elastic sticking plaster to wrap around our pens to stop them slipping out of our fingers as we wrote and rocks to hold down our papers, as the massive steel ceiling fans hanging up above us on the high-ceilinged school hall roof whirled fiercely to try and counteract the heat. Oddly enough I don't remember it being a problem. We sat silently, with the comforting sound of the fans above us, under the gaze of the invigilators who paced up and down between the desks.

After school broke up there were a variety of things to do to while away the summer, the Ladies Recreation Club swimming pool being one of them for us. Sometimes a group of us would go to Shatin on the train, hire bikes from outside the station and cycle around the paddy fields on the banks between them. You saw frogs, newts, snakes, fish and many butterflies on these trips. Shatin was countryside sixty years ago but of course now it's a high rise city!

We often hitchhiked to the beach, or went out on boats, or wandered or cycled around the Peak in the early morning or late afternoon. If you went up the side road past the Dairy Farm building from our flat to Jardine's Corner, crossed the bridge and turned right, you would be at Mount Kellett. I enjoyed cycling the short distance on the path around Mt Kellett; it was sleepy and peaceful. The amahs and cook boys who worked at the large houses there had planted little gardens all along the path, filled with vegetables – and ingenious clacking or flapping machines to scare off the barking deer who crept up at night through the dense undergrowth in the valley to gorge themselves. It was all very calm during the day, but at night the barking deer really barked and were quite noisy.

If you turned left at Jardine's Corner you would almost immediately reach our junior school, Peak School, but before that you would see a little wooden hut with shoes in varying states of disrepair displayed in front of it. Written in wonky letters on a piece of wood propped against this edifice was a sign saying "PINKEE COBBLER".

Pinkee knew all the schoolchildren by sight. He chatted to us as we walked past him, and of course we were often assigned by our parents to take shoes to be mended to Pinkee. He was an industrious man, working from morning till night. He used to wave at us as we cycled past, our damp hair finally being lifted from our faces by the breeze on the downward slope home.

When I was an adult and taking my own children to Peak School I often stopped to talk to Pinkee, still there and still hammering away re-soling the shoes which had such short lives in that climate. You put clean, dry shoes away at night and they were green with mould in the morning. He told me about his successful life. From having nothing but the skill to repair shoes, he had married young, bought his little shack, rented a house and had four children. His eldest daughter had graduated from university, moved on to study further at Massachusetts Institute of Technology and was doing very well in her career. One of his two sons was a doctor and the other was also at university. His youngest child was finishing high school that year. He had bought a house for them all and he now had a van instead of having to walk from the Peak Tram up to his hut every day, carrying his trademark black stained wooden work stand. I never saw him without a calm face or a smile.

Further round the corner from Peak School, along Plantation Road was the Bank Boys quarters. This was a fairly modern building where the young bankers working for HSBC had their billets. They were hardly ever there as far as we children were concerned. When we were out they were working of course and our interest in this building was definitely not the occupants but the slope above the wall from the road. This was actually quite dangerous. We children used to take cardboard boxes up to this slope, climb over the four foot wall from the road, carry our cardboard to the top of the dry, grassy slope and then slide down very fast, hurling ourselves sideways off the cardboard before we hurtled off the wall and onto the road. This was a lot of fun, I can assure you, at least until I was twelve or thirteen and gave it up.

For two years I joined up with about twelve other mid to late teenage pupils to go to canoe camp. This was the highlight of those summer days. The canoes the school hired or borrowed, I don't know which, were kept out in the New Territories; some were more in the style of kayaks and some were heavy wooden double canoes. We would set off towards one or other of the adjacent islands – of which there were ninety-eight, I had learned in Geography with the infamous Mr Vaughan – across the sea, dressed in swimsuits and T-shirts, with very few belongings tucked away out of the wet. Because we were crossing the open sea it was fairly choppy sometimes, so seawater ran down our paddles and we were more or less constantly wet. A great way to remain cool.

Two members of staff accompanied us and led the way. Very often it was a long way, the gaps between the islands being quite large and there were times when we couldn't actually see our destination but only the empty sea. When we reached the designated stopping place we hauled the canoes up onto the beach, unpacked our sleeping bags and bits and pieces – toothbrush, hairbrush, towel, anti-mosquito spray, mosquito coils and matches and a book in my case – and made our way to the government primary school building. Every inhabited island had one and their playgrounds were available for travellers like ourselves.

My father used to go canoeing with his friend Dennis Farrow every summer too, and he had some sweet stories to tell. For instance, the islanders would rig up washing facilities (ie. a bucket) using rope and a shower curtain on the playground by the toilet and then wait outside until Dad and Dennis went in to wash, whereupon they would stare through the lavatory windows or pull aside the curtain to see what these white men looked like. The fact that Dad spoke good Cantonese never crossed their minds.

"Is their hair the same colour both up and down?" they would ponder. "Their arms are red and their body is white! Hi-yah! They have fur on their arms!"

"We want to know how big they are," queried the women. "Are they huge and grotesque like oxen, as people say?" Obviously, Dad being a modest man did not as it were, rise to the occasion.

However, we children didn't have any of this, fortunately. We unpacked the dry items stowed in the teachers' canoe, I can't remember what sort of food it was but I assume things like dried peas and mashed potatoes. These would be augmented with vegetables courtesy of the village headman. Then we rolled out our sleeping bags and settled down on the rough concrete of the playground. I don't think I had one night's sleep for the whole trip, it was so very uncomfortable. During the early hours some of us wandered down to the beach to try and sleep in spite of the sandflies, which required you to wrap yourself in your towels as completely as possible.

Now and again my old friend Leo and I took off in a canoe and idly paddled around on our own.

One night we were doing this in a couple of kayaks and chatting quietly, when a fish the size of a large trout slid down my paddle and flopped around on my lap. Leo tried to get hold of it but it panicked, obviously, and wiggled into the front of the kayak under the canvas and onto my legs. There was nothing for it but for me to get out into the ocean and turn the kayak over. It was fairly daunting, since we were a long away from the shore and it was two in the morning, but the stars were shining brightly and the moon was up so we could see quite well.

I rolled the kayak over and Leo jiggled it around and the fish swam out, thank heavens. We rolled the kayak back up and – I find this hard to believe writing it down now – with no help I climbed back into the righted kayak without another thought. What it is to be young and strong! And thinking of it now, how exciting it was to be there, under the stars in the open sea a long way from anywhere and not to be frightened. Being in the deep ocean was entirely different from being at swimming distance from a beach, but somehow neither of us was particularly alarmed.

It strikes me that there is a lot to be said for our parents' belief in us. We really thought we would be able to cope with things that came along, simply because they themselves thought we would cope and told us we could. I'm still so grateful for their belief in me, since it has been fundamental to me throughout my life.

A HOLIDAY IN JAPAN

Mr YK Yau was a friend and colleague of my father's, though he differed from Dad in three important ways: he was rich, he was young, and he loved all things Japanese. Why he felt so drawn to Japan nobody knew; it was unusual over sixty years ago for a Chinese person to feel that way for obvious reasons, though he was too young to have been personally affected by the Japanese invasion of China, or Hong Kong.

A photo of us at a Japanese restaurant in Hong Kong with Mr YK Yau. My mother is second left, Mr Yau with his arms round Dad, then one of the Japanese ladies standing behind me, sitting next to Dad. I think I was 15.

Whatever the reason Mr Yau, as I always called him, spent some time trying to persuade Dad to join him in his delight in all things Japanese, not very successfully it must be said but very tastily, because we were often invited by Mr Yau to this or that fancy Japanese restaurant as and when they opened in Hong Kong. He kindly included me after I turned fourteen, fortunately for me. I loved sukiyaki$_{32}$ in particular and was extremely happy sitting on the floor, and even more so when white-faced geisha$_{33}$ cooked and served the food in their graceful and stylised manner.

Mr Yau spent a lot of his holidays in Japan, and he discovered a beautiful, reclusive Japanese hotel completely devoid of any foreigners (except him, of course). By this time he had learned some Japanese and was overwhelmed by the beauty, peace and austerity of the hotel's surroundings. He came back to the office and enthusiastically told Dad he wanted to make a booking for our family to go there too, assuring us that he could now get a good deal for us (he was still Chinese, after all) and that he would take it upon himself to arrange our next holiday.

Dad thought why not? The rest of us, "How interesting and exciting!" During the years between going on long leave we had the normal, statutory holidays in Hong Kong: Christmas, Chinese New Year, Easter, summer and various festival holidays such as Ching Ming$_{34}$. YK Yau won his battle and we took our summer holiday in Tokyo for a few days, and then near Nagoya to spend the rest of the week at his wonderful Japanese hotel.

Sixty years ago foreigners were not seen often by regular Japanese people, even in Tokyo, and we discovered we stood out like sore thumbs there. It was quite alarming to me, like being the giant Glumdalclitch who looks after Gulliver after he escapes from the miniature Lilliputians: Japanese women in 1960 struggled to reach four feet ten inches. And there I was, a foot taller with size seven feet. At the top of every escalator in every big Tokyo shop stood a *greeting lady* dressed exquisitely in full costume, bowing deeply to each customer as they slowly arose from the floor below, but they couldn't contain their mirth when they saw me and burst into giggles, clutching their hands over their mouths to control their hysteria. Although I was tall, I was slim and slight for my race so I wasn't amused - it was mortifying and I felt very cross.

Eventually we escaped Tokyo and went off to Nagoya and the peace of Mr Yau's hotel for our few days holiday. The taxi driver was amazed that it was our destination since it was a strictly Japanese hotel but we had a card supplied by Mr Yau, which unequivocally said it was. At the hotel absolutely nobody spoke any English so we had to mime, though fortunately we were expected and met by the beaming and bowing manager.

The hotel was a long, low building with a traditional, up-turned Japanese roof, surrounded by trees and wrapped in a low-lying mist. A large, mirror-calm lake lay beyond it. Everywhere was silent. Tiny ladies in kimonos moved noiselessly out of our way as we followed the hotel clerk to our room. When the door opened, we saw one spacious room with a very large picture window overlooking the lake, from which rose coiling drifts of mist. One or two herons stood motionless by the water. It looked just like a Japanese painting. The hotel clerk indicated that we were to take off all our clothes and place them in a basket, then put on the hotel-supplied kimonos and slippers. The name and logo of the hotel were displayed prominently on both. These would be worn throughout our stay, outside the hotel in the grounds as well as inside. The floor of the room was covered with woven and padded tatami, a sort of soft rattan. It wasn't cold, but on the other hand it was not exactly cosy. We had no way of reclaiming our clothes because they and their basket had been removed and would be carefully laundered for us, ready to be put on again when we left. As for our suitcases, they had been spirited away too, to be stored until or if we should ask for specific items from any of them, which seemed crass somehow.

Mother had cleverly reserved a washbag

with brush, comb and a minimum of other vital necessities thank heavens, although toothbrushes, toothpaste and other items were all supplied in beautiful, individual, patterned cotton bags. I had a couple of books in my handbag, too. Dad had a small beard and moustache, which would have to be tamed by Mum's comb.

The idea of minimalism must surely have come from Japan. There was literally nothing else in our room. I seem to recall perhaps one or two small stools but that may be wishful thinking. The bathroom was equally austere with a miniature tub and basin. We each had a face cloth, and two small towels. I don't remember whether we had a sitting or squatting toilet either. Unlike westerners the Japanese guests used the hotel bathing area and pool rather than independent washing facilities.

We were served meals in our room. The rice paper door with its balsa wood struts slid easily aside and the small items for cooking were brought in by two ladies in kimonos, who knelt at all times. We sat on the floor in a circle around the theatre of action, as little one-ring cookers on stands appeared, plates of delicacies, sauces, ultra-thin slices of Kobe beef and wasabi cabbage, raw eggs, rice, and other items for our meal. Mr Yau must have done the ordering because we were certainly not consulted. The cooking lady's assistant silently handed her everything she needed while she cooked for us without being asked, such was the level of concentration between these two ladies.

Fortunately, we were perfectly adept with chopsticks because there was no other implement provided. We spoke in soft voices, if at all, while accepting each of the many courses, served in small bowls with both hands and a bow of the head from both the chef de cuisine and each of us. We drank any liquid left directly from our bowls before they were re-filled.

After the meal, there was very little to do other than go for a walk around the grounds. It seemed strange to be outside in the evening in nothing but hotel kimonos and the wooden clogs we were provided and which Dad found exceedingly difficult to deal with! He took a ten-and-a-half shoe and I'm pretty sure his clogs were too small because they fitted me. Mother and my younger sisters were fine since they had acceptably-sized feet. On these wooden blocks we teetered along the weaving, decorative paths beneath the damp and dripping trees around the lake, passing a few similarly dressed people to whom we bowed, silently.

Returning to our room and after a short recuperation we were about to play some games when the maids returned. It was dusk. Little, sporadic lights had appeared close to the hotel, but the great lake lay in gathering darkness, the trees outlining its shape in inky patches.

Obviously, it had been decided now was time for bed. The maids on their knees opened simple, slatted cupboard doors and brought out the tatami mats upon which we were to sleep. They unrolled them and laid them in a line across the floor, thereby taking up the entire area of the room. They placed a small pillow and folded white quilted cover, all five perfectly aligned with each other, on each tatami mat and, on their knees, left the room.

We lay down in a row. The half moon rose and shone through the window as we whispered. I happened to land up nearest the window and the sill was low enough for me to see the light of the moon shining on the misty lake – now you see it, now you don't. There was so little crime in Japan that there were no locks on the windows and we were only a few feet above ground level. My absurd imagination convinced me that a samurai$_{35}$ warrior in ancient costume was about to leap onto the window sill brandishing his sword and stand there, legs apart and bent-kneed with his dagger between his teeth, ready to jump into the room and slaughter us all. It made for an uneasy night - at least for me, though Mum and Dad lay blissfully asleep holding hands as always, whilst I watched the moon and the stars appear and disappear in the thin mist.

One thing Mr Yau had insisted upon was us having a traditional Japanese bath and it appeared he had considered our western feelings because without our asking for it – and how could we have done, anyway – the hotel manager had most unusually set aside an hour for us to have the facilities with men excluded, except for Father of course. Thus it was that the following morning, in bright sunshine, we wended our way to the beautiful, large indoor pool with the water reaching right up to the huge windows overlooking the lake.

We were given a basket for our kimonos and a small flannel and towel. We were to go to one of the sets of taps on the tiled wall around the edges of a large, empty tiled area. We had to sit or squat on a small stool and wash ourselves completely using the flannel, and then rinse ourselves from head to foot. Luckily there were a couple of ladies there who took no notice of us at all but whom we watched surreptitiously to find out how to do what we were supposed to do. Having washed, scrubbed and rinsed ourselves it was time to descend into the pool and drift or swim about, Dad keeping a judicious distance from the ladies also there, although they obviously didn't care about him being there at all.

It was wonderful, idly floating about gazing out through the windows over the sparkling lake and seeing the mountains beyond for the first time, since the mist had burned off in the sunshine. The water wasn't just warm, it was hot. I began to see why Mr Yau enjoyed it all so much, it was so easy to float off into a reverie...

However, I suddenly heard Mother behind me, "Mary," she hissed, "don't get too close to that lady over there, she's got a spotty bottom."

Sometimes you had to wonder if some of the magic of life was missed by Mum.

THE WEDDING CAR AND THE AMERICAN SAILORS

Sometimes as I walked past the front of our building I would suddenly have a flashback of Father's pride and joy, his silver Jaguar Mk V, which he had parked there on so many Saturdays, tucked in beside the hibiscus hedge. I can see him now in my mind's eye. Before leaving it, he always wiped his handkerchief over the leaping silver jaguar on the front of its long bonnet.

Saturday in the spring and summer was wedding day at the City Hall Registry Office. After their weddings many a youthful bride and groom would come up on the Peak Tram in their wedding dresses and tuxedos to the top of the Peak. They would stand in groups against the railings of the lookout there and have themselves photographed with the magnificent view of Hong Kong harbour, the mass of Kowloon's buildings and the high green mountains beyond as an unequalled backdrop.

Then they would walk past the car park with hopes of seeing the fabled silver *wedding car*. When they did, they'd clap their hands with delight, whereupon the smart young groom would place his manly foot on the running board, his bride leaning coyly against him clutching her flowers, her veil draped fetchingly over the vehicle. Photos would be taken from all angles. Father took great pleasure in giving these bridal couples this special photo opportunity and I wonder how many wedding albums feature Father's Jag.

One day I climbed the stairs with the heavy bag of books I had to cart with me on my marathon journey to school and back, dumped it on the hall table, kicked my shoes off and buried my feet in the new hall rug, carefully avoiding the dog bones. My eye caught the glory of the old hall rug, risen like a phoenix from the floor and now hanging, resurrected and resplendent from its brass pole and rings on the hall wall, thanks to Mr Surbindar Singh.

Mother was lying on the sofa on the verandah. I grabbed a bottle of water from the fridge and went to join her, slumping in a chair and sticking my feet on the cushions next to hers.

"Did you have a nice day?" she asked.

"Riveting," I sighed, swigging water from the bottle.

"I wish you wouldn't do that."

"Mr Vaughan was in fine form. He decided not to teach us much geography today. He recited *The Owl and the Pussycat* very quietly instead. He says he's not interested in the Great Prairies of the USofA."

"Oh well," said Mother, with her eyes closed.

"They've decided what to do with me about maths, finally."

She opened her eyes, "Yes?"

"Yeah. I'm going to join the D stream and do Maths For The Home. Apparently we're going to measure curtains."

That woke her up.

"And I'll only be able to qualify for a pass."

"But weren't you getting on well with your maths with Dad yesterday?"

"Mum!" I exclaimed, "No way I'm going to ever do those stupid problems! *If one man can mow a field of 1.75 hectares in 2 hours 18 minutes, how long will it take three men to mow a field of 7.4 hectares?*" I intoned.

She blinked.

"Suppose it's raining?" I went on, "Suppose one man's mower breaks down? Suppose one man only had one leg and went round in circles?"

We both laughed.

"I was always so good at maths," she said, wistfully.

"Well, good for you."

We settled back into the peace of the late afternoon, she with her face turned, as always, to the sun.

Outside the windows spread the whole, wide view of the sea, the sun hovering just above the islands dotted around like dark blots on a painting. It was time for the mighty sea-going junks to leave for their night of fishing. Their great dark sails spread as twenty or more of them moved slowly in convoy to the fishing sites, past the islands and out to sea.

We sat up when we heard Dad's voice. Oh dear. He was ushering in some men. Mum and I heaved a sigh in unison. Dad had obviously, once again, felt sorry for some American sailors who had been hanging disconsolately around the top of the Peak Tram and brought them home. We feared as much.

"Come in, come in!" we heard Dad say. "My wife and daughter will be on the verandah."

Two American sailors in their white uniforms appeared at the door. They took their hats off and looked amazed, as if we had sprung from another world. They were blond, solid farm boys, about twenty and just off the warship, which had arrived back from Vietnam that morning for rest and recreation. Dad introduced them as Chuck and Buzz.

Ah Chun bustled in with San Miguel beers and peanuts. They sat down awkwardly but gratefully and seemed, as their comrades so often did, spellbound that there were some real, actual European women there in front of them.

I went to get a gin and tonic for Mum - and incidentally, me. When I returned there was Mum, her blue eyes wide, making effortful conversation: "And so you come from Pinhoe, Iowa, Chuck? Is it very hot?"

"See, Ma'm, it's cold in winter and hot in the summertime."

"And I believe you have very big fields?"

"Oh yes, we do Ma'm."

"Let me see – how many hectares would you say your fields were?"

"Err, Ma'm, we don't measure in hectares."

"Ah. That's a shame. I was going to ask you roughly how long it would take for one man to mow a hectare? Mary's so interested in these conundrums." She said this with a straight face. She was so mischievous, my mother.

Chuck looked dumbfounded, "We don't mow our fields Ma'm, that would take forever!"

"See?" I said.

There was another ring on the doorbell, Ah Chun opened the door and then hurried in.

"Missee! Black man co...!"

Mother held up her hand to stop her as Dad jumped up to greet his newest guest, another American sailor but this time, a black one. He was slight and thin and I noticed his hands; such long, slim fingers. The three sailors nodded to each other, but obviously didn't know each other. Dad asked me to get him a beer but he declined.

"I'll take some wadda please, suh?" he said.

His voice was low and accented. Mother was fascinated: "Where do you come from?" she asked.

"Louisiana, Maam."

"Where there are all the alligators in swamps! And mangroves! And those fat things," I said excitedly. I had poured myself a rather strong gin and it had gone to my head a bit. Boudreaux (pronounced *Boodrow* in Louisiana) for that was his name, laughed, "That's right. And they're called manatees."

Chuck and Buzz were now having a conversation with Mother about varieties of potato in Idaho. She was doing her best to find this subject interesting, poor woman. Dad, on the other hand, had remembered that Louisiana had been French so he asked Boudreaux whether the patois they spoke was similar to the one he was so familiar with from North Africa. Immediately they started speaking French and laughing uproariously.

It wasn't long before Boudreaux's eyes began to wander towards Dad's open grand piano.

"Do you play the piano? Would you like to play?" Dad asked.

"I would!" said Boudreaux, leaping up and walking over to the piano to play a few gentle notes.

Father sat beside him on the piano stool and the two of them began to play gospel songs and spirituals, which then led to Boudreaux playing jazz and Dad playing along a bit with the riffs on the bass. They were having such a great time it was infectious.

Chuck and Buzz stood to leave as they were

going out for hot dogs, but Boudreaux and Dad played on, and my young sister, Sally came and sat on a pouffe beside the piano to listen. After some time and much laughter, the sailor reluctantly said he should go too, although we asked him if he would like to stay for supper. I think he felt he shouldn't impinge on our hospitality any longer, so he followed Dad to the front door. Dad put out his hand to shake his. But instead the young man almost threw himself into Father's arms and hugged him. Dad put his arms around him and I heard him say, as he patted his back, "Come back safe, son, come and see us soon," and, giving him a card he had in his pocket with our phone number on it, he added, "Let us know you're okay, when this war is over."

Boudreaux promised he would. He left, and we all waved goodbye out of the window as he walked away from our building, past the ghost of our *wedding* Jag, and on to the Peak Tram station.

"I hope we hear from him soon, that he's safe," said Dad.

"And the farm boys," said Mum. With that we all went to supper.

But we never heard from Boudreaux again. We don't know if he survived that terrible, pointless war. Whether he lived or died. I'm so glad that he played the piano with Father. Maybe he just didn't contact us because he'd lost Dad's card. Unlike the soldiers, most of the sailors lived.

STORIES OF THE SEA

The sea is everything to us. At midnight we three companions: my boyfriend, our friend and I, let our clothes slide to the cool sand. The light of the moon shimmers across the sea. In our swimsuits wc walk into the silky, still water. We swim slowly, breaststroke, out to the raft moored a fair distance from the beach, enjoying seeing the sparkling green-gold phosphorescence cascading over our arms as we move through the water, barely disturbing the surface.

On the raft we lie stretched out side by side watching the stars above us and whispering our thoughts. Every once in a while one of us stands and dives with barely a splash deep down into the water, to turn quickly and float back up through our own bubbles of phosphorescence, so bright our bodies are outlined clearly as we rise.

After a time we swim back to shore, climb quickly into our clothes and go home. I don't shower. I cover my pillow with a towel to save it from my long wet hair and climb into bed as I am. Our dog Wendy licks the salt off my hands before we both fall into a deep and unmoving sleep.

In the morning on the ferry to school my boyfriend picks up an abandoned newspaper and we both gaze at the headline in a corner of the front page. It reads, "Red Flag Hoisted at South Bay Beach" and says that yesterday multiple sharks were seen in the late afternoon, so swimming was forbidden there until further notice. We stare at each other. Who can see a drooping red flag in the dark, at midnight? We certainly hadn't!

"We were lucky, then," I whisper, while a chill goes down our spines.

Sometimes we like to hitch-hike to a beach at the other end of the island. We have no problem with getting lifts, the ubiquitous small green open-sided lorries, which are used to carry everything in Hong Kong will always pick us up. We sit on the wooden slatted benches on either side in the back behind the cab, surrounded by fishing nets, pots, rope and the plastic bread baskets, which are used to carry everything everywhere.

At Big Wave Bay we leap through and over the waves. We stand in the sea up to our waists as the waves roll in, big waves as the name implies, two or three times our height, our faces alive with exhilaration. With these waves there are several options: we leap up the wave as it approaches and are lifted and carried over its top until we slide down the other side. Or if the wave approaching is already breaking, we have to choose quickly whether we leap or whether we dive straight through it, hoping we will have time to right ourselves in order to make the next leap up the following wave. They come in sevens, but not evenly. Sometimes a wave is breaking too much. The top of the wave is white with foam and curling over to crash upon us before we can dive through it and avoid this – then we take a deep breath and allow ourselves to be scooped up and smashed onto the sandy sea bed as the wave rolls us swiftly, over and over, onto the beach. There we struggle to breathe and stand up against the drag of the sea as it pulls itself out again. We are full of sand; sand in our ears, our hair, our noses. Our swimsuits are heavy, dragged down by the weight of the sand caught in them. We go to the end of the beach and sink into a warm pool there and wash out the sand before we go back to the waves.

Mother sits on the verandah in the late afternoon sun, her face like a sunflower turned to catch the last of its rays. She asks me, "Did you have a nice time?"

"Yes," I say. "We hitch-hiked to Big Wave Bay and jumped around in the waves."

For a moment she hesitates – should she say something about this? Is this dangerous? She decides against it. She likes us to have our freedom. Sometimes I'm a little frugal with the truth, I'm just grateful I don't need to say everything. I'm grateful she mostly chooses not to know.

Father's great friend, the thrice millionaire and twice pauper Mr Ma, who makes fortunes and loses them just as easily, invites us on his super yacht during one of his wealthy incarnations. We are amazed at its beauty, its spaciousness, its luxury! Smartly uniformed crew members cater to our every whim and we play monopoly on the way to Lamma Island, where we are having a fishy lunch and swimming off the boat. There are colourful inflatables on the boat of all sorts: bananas, whales, lilos. We enjoy them all, but we like diving or jumping off the top deck of the boat into the water best.

On the way back in the twilight, just as we spy Stonecutters Island at the entrance to the harbour in the distance, the yacht stops. There is a large sampan with its swaying paraffin lamp lit, bobbing in the water as the fisherman holds on to our rope and bargains with the captain. He is selling crabs. The captain buys five of them, huge greeny-grey monsters. One of the crew hauls up a big bucket of sea water, then kills the crabs by swiftly jabbing the sharp pointed handle of a purple plastic comb between its eyes. They bring the bucket of water to the boil and cook the crabs, crack their shells and bring them, scorching hot, to us where we wait around the table in the stern. I can never forget the taste of these crabs. I will never again have any seafood as good as that.

As youngsters my sister Trudi and I swim out to the raft at Repulse Bay, each carrying our masks and snorkels over one arm. We don't clamber up the ladder and onto the raft; instead we pull the masks over our faces and put the snorkels into our mouths, then we put our heads down into the sea to look under the raft at the myriad fish.

There are black and yellow angel fish, blue striped fish, fish with a big black dot on their shoulders, red fish and blue fish, big fish and small. We don't know the names of the fishes, any more than they do themselves, we just like to be amongst them and watch them. We float around the raft for hours with them. They are unafraid of us; they swim over and under and around us. Now and again we climb onto the raft but the jute cord that covers the surface is quite rough under our softened feet after the silk-smooth sea, so we don't stay on the raft for long. Eventually we see Mother or Father waving at us from the beach and we slowly swim back to join them.

Later, when we are older, my friends and I swim out to the rafts moored at whichever beach we have come to. Once there, we run as fast as possible diagonally across the raft to build up speed – it takes a good six or seven steps – and hurl ourselves in a dive as far as we can go. Our bodies are lithe and strong and we have no fear. It feels like flying. If I close my eyes I know again that invincibility we all have at fifteen or sixteen, born of innocence, ignorance and bodies in their prime. I'm so lucky that I can re-experience such pleasure in the memory of my youthful body, at one with the sea.

Mother floats around or swims side-stroke as long as she's not out of her depth. Father swims breaststroke away from shore in his metronomic fashion, his head popping up with every stroke, in a straight line out and back. Sometimes we all swim together because a dip in the embracing, green-blue South China Sea is a must for all of us.

The sea, after all, is where life began.

THE GOOD OLD DAYS

Ah - the good old days. Where to start? There were so many of them. I remember this day when I was sixteen...

We were the picture of familial peace and harmony. My sister Sally was playing the piano, Mother was humming as she prepared the next English lesson for her friend and student Mrs Beckwith, I was lying on the floor with my legs propped up on the wall as I chatted on the phone and Father was reading the *South China Morning Post*. He shook the newspaper a couple of times, then cleared his throat. Peering over the top of it meaningfully, he then folded it up and looked at Mum with a glint in his eye.

"I've been thinking," he started.

Mum and I paid attention, you had to when he'd been thinking. I told my friend I would phone him back as there was something interesting in the offing.

"Thel, why don't we have a party for your fortieth birthday?"

"But darling! I thought we said we'd go to Macau for the weekend...?"

"How about," continued Dad as we listened with bated breath, "we have a treasure hunt!

And hide clues all over town and people can go around searching for them from place to place...?"

I felt enthusiastic. "You mean in cars, Dad? Or on foot?"

"Oh cars, darling! And we should make everyone collect something to prove they've actually been there and read the clue..."

"Sounds fun!" said I.

"Can I do it?" implored Sally from the piano stool.

"Oh. But I don't really..." said Mother

"I've started writing the clues," continued Dad, "in rhyming couplets."

"I see," said Mum.

Our Father was very good at doggerel. He had a natural flair for it. He said it was because he was a Londoner. He loved creating them, he couldn't help himself. Sometimes it verged on poetry. Every single wedding anniversary he wrote a poem summarising the year, for Mum. There are sixty-seven of them. So there really was no stopping him once he had the idea.

Good Old Days The Rotten Lot in the early stages of party mode.

Our parents had an exceptionally close group of friends known, curiously, as The Rotten Lot. They were based around the Union Church, to which our parents had gravitated when they first arrived in Hong Kong and where Dad had relatively recently become a Deacon. The Rotten Lot were mostly Scots, and quite a few were based at the famous Tamar Dockyard - and a free and easy and immensely fun lot they were, too.

The Rotten Lot enjoyed themselves. They loved to dance every Monday to Scottish Country Dancing and when Mother had discovered Nip's Dancing School they were very glad to strut and sway there to the likes of the pasodoble or the rumba. The idea, therefore, of Dad distributing his clues around the city for their friends to rush around searching for in harem-scaram fashion didn't seem totally outlandish to them.

Good Old Days The Rotten Lot in the early stages of party mode.

On the Saturday afternoon of the party Mum and Dad drove off to plant the clues Dad had wrought in their open top two-tone Zephyr Zodiac, planning to sellotape his witty little ditties to various notable buildings or statues around the city. Meanwhile at home, Ah Chun was overseeing the chef and the waiter who had been hired for the evening from the Ladies Recreation Club to help at the party. I invited my boyfriend of the time who was often bemused by my parents, but though he may have thought them somewhat eccentric he enjoyed joining in with them when he could.

The plan was that everyone would start the race after a glass of Champagne and the delivery of the first clue. Every couple was given the written clue together with a small bag to collect the various trophies in. I remember one clue, stuck discreetly in the corner of a door into the Communist Bank of China, was accompanied by a little container of non-viable one cent notes as *treasure* trophies. Apparently these notes were only printed because they were needed by accountants to balance corporate books and I imagine Father was amused to assign such worthless pieces of paper to the Chinese Communist Party.

But the most memorable clue, surely, had to be at Victoria Park. Somehow Mother had managed to sellotape the clue right up behind the royal ear of the statue of Her Majesty Queen Victoria. My boyfriend and I were being driven in a foursome, so as soon as the couple we were with drew up we rushed to the huge black statue on its vast granite plinth. We clambered up the Queen to scramble all over her mighty and forbidding bosom to reach our goal. Balancing ourselves by holding on to the Queen's supercilious nose we managed to read the clue to the next destination. Mother was an athletic woman as this demonstrated! And I think the trophy in the bag there was, suitably, a tiny royal blue plastic flower.

Finally, after much driving up and down and hilarity when meeting or overtaking our rivals, not to mention being under pressure to get everywhere first, we all arrived back at my parents' home to great applause - and somebody won something, I have no idea who or what. That wasn't the point anyway. The Ladies Recreation Club waiter, who knew Mother fairly well since she was a long term member, handed around cocktails and small chow snacks. Soon afterwards part two of Father's birthday plan began.

He had put a collection of directives into his top hat to be picked out by each couple, and which had to be followed to the letter. Soon everyone was milling about doing their best to obey. One of these diktats I recall instructed Eva and Alec to wind a complete roll of toilet paper around the legs of the grand piano, while Joan and Alec were informed that on no account should toilet paper be wound around the piano legs. Moreover, the toilet paper must not be torn by either contestant. Hence, they were all on the floor under the piano, laughing. So was I, watching them. And so it went on, with more ridiculous games. Later, we had a delicious dinner cooked by the club chef. Then, since we had so much space in our flat with its polished parquet flooring, there was music and dancing until the not so early morning. And that was how Mother celebrated her big four-oh.

Since so many of the Rotten Lot were Scots, at New Year - or Hogmanay - the party at wherever the Rotten Lot had chosen to enjoy themselves continued through the night and included breakfast, to which I most certainly came. In fact my friends and I sometimes left our own parties to come home when my parents hosted one, to share in the fun they always had.

Ah well. Those were the good old days. Thank you Mum and Dad for all the fun and happiness you gave us.

SETTING SAIL FOR JAPAN

Father loved long distance travel so he was fortunate, as were we, that he could indulge his passion. Dad's contract, even years after his first posting, still gave the family six months *home leave* every two-and-a-half years on full salary, and travel back *home* first class by P&O liner for all five of us. Or we could take the equivalent money and do what we liked with it for six months. Hah! No guessing what Dad chose to do.

As soon as we returned from one *leave*, Dad was there on the floor with his atlas planning our next tortuous adventure.

"So what do you think, Thel? Shall we go to Japan first, then Mexico, then New Orleans? Or do you think...?"

Mum smiled, "You decide darling, I don't mind," she said, and she didn't. She was happy to go wherever he chose, not because she didn't have a mind of her own but because she believed he would make the right decisions and relied on him to do so.

Although once he slipped up, when I was seventeen. Poor Mrs Mackenzie at Jardines Travel! No sooner had she washed her hands of Miller Travel Extravaganza part three or four, than she had to welcome, no doubt with a sinking heart, Father bouncing back through her door with his latest scheme. At least she had two years to work on the worldwide bobbing and weaving Dad thought up. This particular trip began with us catching a Dutch cargo ship to Japan, sailing across the Pacific to Los Angeles, flying to Mexico City for a week, then on by Mexican propeller plane(!) over the mountains to Guadalajara.

Nobody had thought about my A-Levels. They had blithely booked for us all to leave on the Dutch boat several days before the end of the exams, so I would have been spirited away exactly when I was supposed to be sweating buckets in the school hall over A-level biology.

"Hey!" I said, "I have to do my exams!"

They looked shocked.

"Errr.. well, maybe they could send them to us on the ship?"

"No!" I cried, outraged, "I have to be here! In school!"

"Oh, I know," declared Mum, relieved, "We'll go on and you can stay with the Van Diepens, and then fly to Tokyo and pick us up there."

As I thought I was in love and didn't want to leave anyway, I was happy to acquiesce. I knew the Van Diepen's well and was delighted to stay with them since it meant my boyfriend and I would have some extra days together, which at seventeen seemed worth any sacrifice, particularly one of sitting on a cargo ship with my parents.

All went swimmingly, as they say, until the night before the flight, when a typhoon blew up. It was the summer and typhoon season. Mrs Van Diepen, the boyfriend and I had a crazy time with the flight being on again/off again and driving through the cross-harbour tunnel to the airport to find the plane cancelled, so driving all the way back home up the Peak. Mrs VD got fed up – she was not a patient lady – and decided to phone the airline, cancel my flight, send a message to my parents on board the ship and re-schedule me for the following day. This she did. Boyfriend and I had a smoochy evening and the next day I caught the plane to Tokyo. Perfect.

What no one in Hong Kong knew was that a series of unfortunate events had occurred in Japan. First of all, the ship had finished offloading its cargo in Tokyo earlier than expected and the captain decided to move on to the port of Yokohama. So off my family went, unworried as always and Dad would come back up to Tokyo to collect me, which he duly did. Unfortunately, he didn't get the message from Mrs Van Diepen that I wasn't on the planned plane. Nearly sixty years ago nobody spoke much English in Japan and somehow the message had been lost. Even more bizarrely Dad checked several times at the airline desk that Miss M Miller was on said plane and was assured that she was.

Everyone came through arrivals but I wasn't there. He couldn't believe I was missing.

"Yes," the Japanese airline lady said again, "Miss Miller has arrived."

"But she hasn't!" declared Dad.

The lady nodded enthusiastically, "Yes, she here but now she left airport."

This was a bit of a body blow to poor Father. Where had I gone? There were no such things as mobile phones and the typhoon had blown out the telephone lines on the Peak. In pursuing this conundrum he then discovered an American family called Miller with an M initialled daughter, had in fact arrived and had indeed presumably left the airport. And as there were several more planes coming in at odd times that night because of the disruption from Hong Kong, Dad had to meet all of them, standing miserably at Arrivals and not seeing me come out, again and again.

Meanwhile, the ship with Mother and sisters on it had completed unloading the small amount of cargo for Yokohama, so the jaunty captain told Mum they would now be sailing on to Nagoya - but not to worry, the trains were fast to Nagoya, Dad and I could join them there. Mother was not overjoyed at this news, since she couldn't let Dad know the destination had changed and she didn't know why we hadn't turned up at Yokohama, either. Off steamed the ship carrying

Mother and girls around Japan to Nagoya while at last - and twenty-four hours late - I innocently arrived in Tokyo with my big, heavy pigskin leather suitcase, to be clutched to my Father's bosom as if I had risen from the dead.

Finally, Dad managed to get the airline to contact Mrs Mackenzie, the travel agent in Hong Kong, who communicated with the shipping line, who sent a message to the captain of the ship to tell him we were still in Tokyo. He messaged back telling us to come to Nagoya. Dad replied we would do as instructed as soon as possible. Mother was no doubt relieved to hear this.

The trains in Tokyo are amazing and even in the 1960s we swooped into the city from the airport on the monorail, which was exciting. However, Tokyo Central was packed, there were so many trains it was bewildering and absolutely nothing was written in English. With the help of a student we finally managed to buy a ticket to Nagoya on the express train. It was leaving in ten minutes from platform twenty-two but like everything numerical in Japan there was no actual rhyme or reason to the layout of the numbers. We kept saying, "Nagoya?" to people who stared at us, laughing behind their hands at the incomprehensible sounds these Europeans were making. We dashed about frantically but eventually someone pointed us in the right direction. We ran like mad creatures, hauling my suitcase behind us, and managed to jump on the train.

It was not what we had anticipated, not whizzy as we had been led to expect of the express. It bumbled off at exactly the scheduled moment and stopped shortly afterwards at a suburban station. Then on it rumbled, laden with *salarymen* and stopping every few minutes to let them out. It dawned on us that we were on the wrong train and nobody seemed to know whether its destination was Nagoya or somewhere else.

Dad was not easily defeated. He continued asking all and sundry for help in English and French for good measure, until a bespectacled middle-aged man replied that the train was indeed going to Nagoya but would take many hours. No, he said, certainly it was not the express! Did it look like the express? The express was on the opposite side of platform twenty-two - the special express side! The express had *Express* written on its side, in English! He shook his head, how could we have missed it?

Dad managed to persuade this gentleman to telephone the Port Authority at Yokohama when he got off the train to explain that we were on our way and ask them to hold the ship. The man had obviously never dreamt of doing anything so outrageous in all his life, but Dad thrust a wodge of US dollars at him to pay for the call as we arrived at his stop.

We had no way of knowing whether he had phoned, or if the Port Authorities would hold the ship. But we trundled on hopefully through the Japanese countryside as evening set in. We later found he had indeed phoned, thus acquiring an extraordinary anecdote about crazy Europeans to tell family and friends, while quaffing his saki.

Meanwhile, back at the ship the now somewhat less than jaunty captain and his crew had finished off-loading several hours earlier and couldn't understand why we hadn't arrived at Nagoya as they were more than ready to leave. The weather was fair across the wide ocean, and now was the time to set sail - so sorry, Mrs Miller, said the captain, but we will have to haul up the hawsers[36] and go...

Only Mother would not allow it. How she had prevented them leaving before this I don't know, surely even the power of her considerable charms must have started to wane? She was absolutely determined, however, not to set sail across the Pacific without Dad. Or me, I presume. The captain grew more and more frustrated and said, "Look, we have waited for them for hours, days, we have to leave, we are late already and we have a schedule!"

At this point the captain told the sailors to pull up the gangway. Without hesitation, before they could do so Mother stepped onto it, walked halfway down it and stood firm. What were they to do? The Indonesian sailors were not about to pick up Mother in her flower-sprigged, full-skirted dress and carry her struggling back up the gangplank, and the officers were not going to manhandle any female passengers and potentially lose their jobs and risk their careers! Stalemate.

Back to Dad and me. We had finally arrived at Nagoya station and found a taxi, which by dint of wavy-sea hand gestures we pressured into taking us to the port. Having got there we had to show our passports to get through the gates. Thank goodness, we thought we have our passports so all will be well! We produced them with a flourish.

But no. The Port Authorities became peculiarly agitated when they inspected our passports, then sternly informed us that we were illegal. We didn't have the relevant visitor's visa. Without this permit stamped in our passports we were persona non grata. In fact we could not be there standing in front of them. It was only possible for us to be on board a ship. So it was impossible for us to have been wandering around Japan willy-nilly.

"Oh, let us through, we're trying to leave!" importuned Dad. "Look, we'll get on that ship and be gone!"

We stared longingly at the big blue ship lurking unattainably at the far end of the dock.

But Father's pleas changed nothing. To set foot on Japanese soil we must have a visa.

Without a visa how could we be in Japan? As far as they were concerned we were not in Japan and we were not approved persons to enter the port as, all evidence to the contrary, we could not exist.

"You cannot be in Japan," they said flatly.

But there we undeniably were, living, breathing persons. What a conundrum. Men were on telephones. Men raised their voices. Men grew tense.

Then suddenly, out of the blue, two people in black leather with brass epaulettes, fancy logos and black zigzag helmets roared up on motorbikes.

"Get on!" said one of them tersely. Dad pushed me onto the front bike and flung my case across my lap, nearly crushing me. He jumped onto the one behind and we immediately zoomed off with a squeal and loud pops of exhaust for the five minutes it took to get us to the ship. And there was Mother standing halfway down the gangway, with my sisters looking perplexedly over the railings above.

"Here they are!" declared Mother to the captain as we clambered off the motorbikes.

"Go! Go!" shouted the policemen, because that was who they turned out to be, "You are not allow in Japan! Don't come in Japan without visa!"

"We certainly won't," Dad assured them, shoving me up the gangway and lugging my suitcase behind him.

"Well done!" said Mum and Dad admiringly to each other, holding hands on the deck at the top of the gangway as the sailors hauled it up. The Captain slapped Father on the back, and the ship blew its three farewell blasts before pulling out to sea.

"Come for a drink, Dusty?" asked Dad's friend Eddie Wu, and off they went to their favourite bar.

"I want to ask you a favour," said Eddie, once they'd settled down."

"I'm not joining your poker club, if that's what you're after – it's far too high stakes for me!" said Dad.

Eddie was typically Chinese, a born gambler. Eddie laughed, "No, no. That's not it! I'm not crazy. But aren't you going to the US on leave very soon?"

Dad was curious. "Yes, in about three weeks. Why?"

"Good," continued Eddie, "because I've got a suggestion to make, and yes, it is to do with the poker club."

"What's happened?" asked Dad uneasily. Eddie was a very rich man who played for big money, and Dad was unwaveringly a *top bet of a fiver* man.

Eddie took a deep drag on his cigar. "This'll surprise you, Dusty," he smiled, "but a week ago I won a house."

"At poker?" cried Dad, aghast.

"Yes. Only it's in California. A place called St Helena. Sixty miles from San Francisco - I believe it's very nice around there? Obviously I haven't seen it..."

"Good heavens!"

"It's a very big house," continued Eddie apologetically. "It's in the woods, apparently. It has a big swimming pool as well. Five bedrooms and three bathrooms."

"What's this got to do with me?" asked Dad, gulping his beer.

"My nephew Joseph lives in San Francisco, only he's married to an American woman who's acting a bit strangely at the moment! I thought he'd want to drive down and have a look, see what needs doing to it to secure it – you know. He's got the keys. But they have an eighteen month old and some new twins apparently, and it seems she doesn't want to go - or let him go, either."

"So...?"

"So, Dusty my friend. Joe could meet you in the city and give you the keys and directions, and you could go and have a holiday in the house for a couple of weeks and check it over? What do you think?"

So that is what we did. We met Joe and collected the keys and met his, according to Eddie, strangely pale and exhausted American wife and the three babies. They were charming. The babies were two or three weeks old, sweet but demanding; Joe's wife didn't say much because she spent all her time feeding them. I thought, no way am I ever going to land myself up with babies! Odd how a few years changes your perspective but even so... three of them in eighteen months?

We hired a flashy car, which seemed enormous and lush to us, although I have since been told by American friends it was actually small and ordinary to them. It was a light blue metallic Dodge Dart and we felt a million dollars as we drove down the wide American roads to St Helena, our vast amount of luggage stowed in the boot, strapped to the roof, scattered around the back seat and some smaller bits shoved under Mum's feet.

The house was indeed in the countryside, up a long, winding, unmade drive. It nestled in the trees completely alone and looking deserted. Everyone but me was thrilled with it! But for me its isolation was my worst nightmare.

We dumped the baggage and looked round the house, built in three wings around a pool. The main house stretched across the top, with wide glass sliding doors and two wings on either side, which had verandahs all along them. In the centre of this three-sided house was the very large and beautiful swimming pool. The huge trees shadowing much of the house rustled in the breeze and birds filled the air, squawking and singing.

We emptied the car and jumped back into it to drive down the road to the little town of St Helena. Never had I seen such large people! Their broad bottoms filled their tartan pedal pushers straining the seams; their trolleys were full of food we had never seen before and didn't realise you could even buy. Every woman was chewing gum and appeared to be buying multiple gallon containers of milk and quart bottles of Coca-Cola, frozen orange juice, cheesecake, waffles and maple syrup. Mother swiftly turned into a diminutive St Helena everywoman. She, too, excitedly filled her trolley with full-fat milk, cheese, cereals and fast foods of varying sorts but then her thrilling binge ended as she searched around for any vegetables she could find - sprouts, broccoli, courgettes, anything – but there were few. Corn on the cob, iceberg lettuce, tomatoes and frozen peas were all I seem to remember.

Back we went to the house. Everyone jumped in the pool. Mum cooked something. It was lovely. But as the evening set in and it grew darker the deer came down to the house and walked around it, their hooves clicking on the gravel, scaring the life out of me. You may wonder what was the matter with me and why I was, unlike everyone else, so unhappy in the house? It was because for a couple of years my friends and I had been fixated on watching The Untouchables[37]. There were four seasons of The Untouchables featuring the brutal and inscrutable policeman, Eliot Ness. It was filmed very realistically and the action was unrelentingly gruesome and violent. In the series Eliot Ness cruised around Chicago and environs between 1959 and 1963, and the episodes were based on the experiences of the real aforesaid Ness. It was narrated as well as acted so it was as if you were seeing it actually happening and thus it was very believable - especially since it was all in fact true.

So in 1964, aged 17, here I was in a remote American house, which had been empty for some time, surrounded by woods and which was exactly the sort of place that Eliot Ness's evil gangs would hide themselves, stash their loot, bury their multitudinous and tortured victims' bodies and commit further dastardly and unimaginably horrible crimes. I suspected Eliot Ness's monsters were hiding in every dark corner, under every bush, masquerading as pine trees, lurking about everywhere and if not here at this very minute, about to return soon. I explained my fears to Father.

"Don't be silly!" he sighed, exasperated. "It's perfectly fine! It's lovely! Don't worry so much, darling! It's completely off the beaten track!"

"But that's the point, Dad! They choose remote places! We should take turns being on watch!"

Dad rolled his eyes, "For heaven's sake. Go

and have a swim and leave it to me."

But I couldn't leave it to him. He and Mum were oblivious to the danger. They had never watched Eliot Ness, how could they know?

The following morning we all had cornflakes with the rich American full fat milk and they tasted delicious! I ate two bowlfuls. Everyone else seemed quite able to digest it but I, having only drunk the watery Hong Kong Dairy Farm milk or equally watery powdered stuff, which I disliked intensely, almost all my life, vomited it up copiously. It took me forty years or so to eat cornflakes again. I was not having a nice time.

But I digress. During the day we walked out of our bedrooms into the sunshine, dropped our nighties on the ground and dived into the pool. It was blissful swimming around entirely on our own. We went for trips in our flashy blue metallic Dodge Dart and for walks around the area. We girls and Mum played for hours on massive swings hooked onto amazing, tall trees so that you felt you were flying with the birds and we ate the American hamburgers and meat loaf that we'd bought, which we covered with mayonnaise and tomato sauce in the American way. McDonald's and the other ubiquitous American fast food chains had not yet penetrated our Hong Kong world.

But night was a different matter altogether. Every night I fetched the bread knife from the kitchen and began my guard duty. I prowled the perimeter, fearful but determined that if any lookalike Eliot Ness or his cohorts should appear to collect their ill-gotten gains hidden in this remote house and thereby threaten my family, they would have to fight me first, which would give Dad time to wake up. I remember looking through the open window of my parents' room and seeing them blissfully asleep without a care in the world and feeling grimly mollified that at least they were getting some rest.

At dawn I climbed into bed and slept like a log for three or four hours, to be woken by squealing and splashing and people eating cornflakes, the thought of which made me gag. This nightly duty continued for the entire two weeks, with my heart skipping a beat every time a branch dropped or a deer moved around. I told Mum and Dad about it as we drove back to San Francisco in the Dodge Dart and they were more irritated than grateful, but I have never been gladder than to get to Los Angeles, even though we had to wait around in the busy airport since we'd missed the plane to Mexico City. But that's another story.

Still, Eddie Wu was grateful and everyone else was happy, so I suppose it was a success.

AMERICA - DETROIT

When we got to America we discovered something surprising... In some ways it seemed more alien to us than India or Japan.

It had been a challenge to haul all five of us around the United States with our multitudinous suitcases and bags. Mother had found it necessary to bring three or four pieces of luggage just for herself and I had even had to remove my teddy bear from my own case to fit in more of her shoes. I didn't entirely resent this but it did mark out a shock growing-up moment in my life. The first time I had gone anywhere without my teddy bear, but I also agreed that it was about time I did so, being seventeen.

Our parents, early in our time in Hong Kong, had had made an elegant but solid, matching collection of brown pigskin leather suitcases. They looked impressive in an Agatha Christie sort of way. We each had a case – Mother had two - and matching vanity cases, which were square with a handle on the top. The whole collection was made to withstand storage in the hold of a ship in rough weather, with hand-stitched reinforced corners and thick leather handles. By the time we got to America they were splattered with various colourful stickers from a variety of shipping lines.

This was all well and good for ships. Carting the massed collection of them through airports and Greyhound bus stations was a whole different ball game – they weighed a tonne. They had to be carried, they had no wheels. And there were a lot of them, including Mother's hatbox.

At one point we arrived in Detroit to catch a Greyhound bus to Richmond, Ontario to stay with Grandad and our Canadian Granny. It was late and dark and all the porters were on strike. The bus station was cold and cavernous and people were scuttling around silently. We were exhausted; we had just flown up from Mexico. Just recalling it all now makes me wilt.

Mother sat on a bench surrounded by luggage, with Sally and Trudi who were nine and thirteen, while Dad hurried off to buy tickets and try to find anyone at all with any information. The scheduled departure time was looming. I couldn't move the massed suitcases piled up on the floor in front of us on my own and it seemed dangerous to split up and leave anything unguarded anyway. The atmosphere was uneasy, with an undertone of threat.

The strike meant every trolley was chained up and unusable, while all the black porters leaned against the wall in a group, watching. Across the hall I could just see Dad's head in a queue at the ticket office. From the distance he caught my eye and held up three fingers. Obviously, we had to get to bus station 3.

But how? I said to Mum we would have to get a porter somehow. Sally was asleep leaning on her shoulder.

Suddenly, I got one of those bursts of confidence, energy and irritation that hit you out of the blue. I hurried over to the group of lounging porters, who seemed exceedingly surprised to see me, blonde haired and tall as I was.

"Hallo," I said, "are you porters?"

They looked at each other. "We're on strike."

"I realise that - but I need a porter, so could one of you kindly come? Please," I added. I gestured to Mum, in the middle of our pile of luggage. A tall, thin man with a toothpick in his mouth pushed himself off the wall and stared at me.

"I said, we're on strike!" he repeated.

"But I need a porter!"

"You ain't American," he stated.

"No, I'm not, and I'm not getting a very good impression of Americans so far, either! So could someone kindly help me? I have to get all these cases to gate 3."

"She ain't American," repeated the thin guy. "Seeing as how you ain't American I kin help you just this one time, cos you makin' me laugh 'n mebbe I ain't on strike against no foreigners." The assembled group sniggered.

"Good. Well, come on then," I said and hurried back to Mum. The bemused porter hesitated, then collected a trolley and followed. We loaded the baggage together and wheeled it to gate 3.

"Could you keep an eye on all this stuff for me, please? Because I have to go over to my Dad," I said. He gave me an indecipherable look. I waved at tired Mum and my sisters sitting on their bench far across the hall, Mum holding her jewellery case tightly on her lap, then I left the porter and hurried to get some money to pay him from Dad.

A white man in his forties was standing next to Dad in the queue.

"That was dangerous," he said to me. I was startled, "What was?"

"Accosting them black guys."

"I didn't 'accost' anyone!"

"Listen here, don't you go talking to no black guys in Detroit, okay?"

"What are you talking about? They're porters!"

Dad winked at me. "I'm coming, I'm getting the tickets, go back," he said. So I did.

The porter was waiting with everything still on the trolley, chewing on his toothpick.

"Oh gawd!" I said with some asperity, since people were already putting their bags into the hold of the bus. "We need to unload all this quickly! Come on!"

"Where you from?" asked the non-porting porter.

"Hong Kong," I said. He looked nonplussed.

"Are they all like you there?"

"I'm English."

"Oh man."

"Look, let's get this into the bus and then you can get back to leaning on your wall." He burst out laughing and so did I. He started hauling the suitcases off his trolley, which is when Dad turned up, all smiles, waving the tickets.

"Fantastic!" said Dad, smiling at the porter who had now unloaded the last item. "We could never have managed without you!" He stuck out his hand to shake the porter's, who looked amazed but shook it.

The bus driver climbed aboard the huge vehicle. Dad paid the porter, who stared at the variety of what seemed identical green notes in his hand in wonder.

"Thanks for being so helpful," Dad beamed at him, whereupon the porter helped Mum and Sally onto the bus.

Then he said, "You ain't like the folks round here." He shook his head and went off to join his strikers.

"What was that all about?" Dad asked me when we'd sat down.

"They're on strike."

"Ummm... so that was nice of him, helping you - I thought he looked a bit sad."

"Maybe. I don't know Dad, I just want to go."

"Here we go then! Off to Canada!" He squeezed my knee in the ultra-irritating way he had. The bus roared to life and as it drove slowly past the porters, they raised their hands unsmilingly and waved us goodbye.

RIOT

I'm in another place, another time, another life. I'm standing in the Challenge Bookshop, Union House Arcade in Central, Hong Kong. I am nineteen years old and I'm the assistant manager of this small bookshop. It is after lunch on an autumn Friday in 1966, and we have no customers. Although we are at work, the shoppers have stayed away because of threats of riots on the streets. Now though, we know the threat is real and the riots are coming our way because a policeman has just rushed through the arcade to tell everyone, and he tells us that we are safer to stay where we are.

I am feeling very anxious. The two Chinese girls who help in the bookshop, Theresa and Pandora, are making me even more worried because they are almost paralysed with fear and I feel responsible for them. Theresa is intermittently sobbing and holding on to me, while Pandora is speechless and her features are drawn almost into a rictus. They are good Christian girls.

The phone rings, and it is my father.

"Hallo - Mary," he says urgently. "Mr Woo just phoned. The rioters are coming down past the Hilton now, he's barricaded his family in the back and wound down the shutters. Lock the door, turn out the lights and get upstairs into the cockloft." Mr Woo is an old friend of my Dad's.

"What?" I say.

"Just turn the lights out, get upstairs and hide in the bookshelves. They've smashed the big windows, the Hilton windows..."

Pandora makes a small wailing sound.

"I can't get to you, I'm getting off the phone, I'm not far away, get upstairs!"

"But it's completely dark upstairs Dad without the lights!"

"Try not to worry too much darling," replies Dad, "I'm watching from here. Get in the cockloft." He rings off. His office is barely half a mile away in the government offices at Murray Building up Garden Road - so near and yet so far! He can't help us. His friend Mr Woo, from Woo Chang Kee the jewellers round the corner from me with whom he often drinks tea, has warned us but it seems he is hiding in his shop behind locked doors, so he is out of reach as well.

I say to the girls, "Quick, let's lock everything here and the back service door too."

So we rush to lock and bolt the front door and I roll down the blinds. Theresa locks the back. They both quietly but continuously weep; they are small and slight and protectively brought up; maybe they are just as afraid of being gang-raped as being killed.

In pitch darkness we clamber up the spiral staircase to the cockloft where the books are stored. We stumble through the newly delivered boxes, which only yesterday I was enjoying unpacking, smelling the paperbacks' new paper smell, excited to rediscover what I had ordered from Penguin two months earlier...

We hide behind some unopened boxes at the back of the loft, between shelves. It's completely dark. We don't have a phone line up here so we sit on the floor behind the boxes holding hands and I try to stop them – and myself - weeping as we have to be very, very quiet. We can hear the noise of the rioters; it seems they are in the arcade now. I squeeze the hands of the frightened girls in warning and suddenly we all become completely silent. I am just as frightened as they are. Outside we can hear shouts and crashing; they are getting nearer and nearer and it sounds like they are shattering windows. I am afraid they might hear the thudding of our hearts from outside, so frightened are we, and then decide to hunt us out.

Nothing can prepare a woman for the overwhelming shock of a crazed, adrenaline-fuelled mob of hundreds of men. They are beyond frightening. You can actually smell a mob, full of testosterone. We shake in our hiding place while they make their way through the arcade; we hear the crash as they smash the windows of the shop next door, the noise fills us with dread. Pandora sighs in resignation and whispers, "We will die" and buries her head in my shoulder.

"No!" I whisper back. "We won't!" But of course how can I be sure? People have, and do.

The rioters rampage up and down outside our shop for what seems hours. The noise is terrifying; the shouting, the fury, the intermittent high pitched shrieking and the crashing of wooden poles against the windows and doors of the arcade. Then just when I really think I will pass out with the intensity of our joint fear, it seems I can hear them less well. Theresa and I sit upright and strain our ears like dogs in the dark.

"Are they going?"

"I think so."

We remain perfectly still for some minutes. Pandora lifts her head from my shoulder. Theresa lets go of my hand and the three of us lean back against the big boxes of books. We can still hear them and by mutual instinctive consent we stay where we are, straining to listen, our bodies periodically shaking from head to foot in reaction. We decide they definitely are moving away. Then we hear running feet. Some people seem to be chasing after the rioters. We stay still. After a time they, too, are gone.

In Queen's Road Central, outside Union House, Chinese martial music starts to blare from the top of the Bank of China. In response, the Government Information Services building almost opposite it starts up its own cacophony; they have brought up to their roof a number of huge speakers and the noise is terrible. They are playing the William Tell overture at hundreds of decibels.

I take a deep breath. "We don't need to be so frightened now, do you think?" I ask the girls.

We still don't move. Pandora starts to tell us about her family's horrible experiences in China before they managed to flee to Hong Kong, and it is grim to hear. It's no wonder they are so petrified; I put my arms around her and hug her. Somehow none of us wants to leave this darkness, this cocoon, which has become a haven of safety, a female womb in the heart of an alien tide of violence. We sit still and whisper to each other.

After a little while I hear the phone ring; of course it must be Father. With difficulty I crawl across the floor, crashing into the various boxes, and finally find the handrail of the spiral staircase. There are no lights on within the arcade, either, but I find the phone on the desk. He sounds shaky and his love and fear for me pour down the phone line, they're almost tangible.

"Are you all right?" he asks.

"Yes Dad."

"Good girl," he says in a tight voice. "Wait there for half an hour to be safe, but you could put the lights in the back on now, I think. I'll come down then. You've been a brave girl, darling."

"Dad..." I start to say, but I can find no words.

It was then I decide to go to Australia.

But only for a short time. I couldn't bear to be away from home for long.

THE SHIP

I sat on the hard wooden bench and stared out of the window of the Star Ferry as it battled its way across Hong Kong harbour from Kowloon. Rain lashed down and the wind was howling round the boat. I heaved a sigh of relief that I'd actually caught it because it could well be the last before Typhoon Sandy arrived in full force. Through the rain I looked at the Royal Hong Kong Yacht Club before the heavy rain obliterated it from view. Here I was, back in Hong Kong after six months of living and working in Sydney and so very happy to be home in time for Christmas.

The ferry docked and everyone waited as it bounced up and down, while the sailors tried to lower the gangway. Finally, we passengers struggled off the boat. It was useless to use an umbrella, or even to try to remain dry in a typhoon as I well knew from experience. Everything was so familiar - the atmosphere, the air, the smell, the vibrancy and the wealth that was obvious all around. That indefinable Hong Kong thing that was impossible to label and impossible to miss. I felt a familiar bubble of excitement in my throat.

It was pouring, so I decided to duck into a

cafe and settle down with a coffee and a piece of cheesecake to wait it out. I really didn't want to queue for a taxi in this rain. As I sat there drinking the coffee I couldn't help thinking of the Yacht Club and the ridiculous things we had all done when we were younger. Like the event with the American ship. I laughed aloud as I thought of it.

Who had been there that day? I tried to remember. Certainly Loretta Lo and Amelia *Meeli* Chisholm because they were never apart, not since they had started Glenealy School together at the age of four. And Jimmy Alvares because it was his yacht. Also Tom. And the wonderful, fascinating Henry Neeves, guitarist and eccentric who at the time had taken to wearing a Carnaby-style pink denim suit with a waistcoat more or less constantly. And me, of course.

I sipped the coffee and found I'd finished it, so I signalled the waiter who came over and I ordered a glass of wine.

So... Jimmy and Tom had taken Jimmy's little racing boat out that morning, I remembered, and by the time I arrived at the club the two boys were well into the racing and buzzing around all over the harbour in the blazing sunshine. Meanwhile the rest of them were drinking beer, munching crisps and telling stories, which caused periodic bursts of loud laughter. We all watched the end of Jimmy's race, which he won, so he and Tom were in high spirits when they joined the rest of us.

"It's a pain in the neck, though," Tom said, "that damn great American aircraft carrier is taking up so much space, it interferes with the racing."

We all looked out of the big window across the harbour where the USS Enterprise$_{38}$ was moored. It did indeed take up what appeared to be half the harbour. It was massive, not just long but very wide because of the wing-like decks where numerous planes were lined up in rows. I disliked anything to do with the war; I couldn't imagine the number of bombs the Americans had dropped on the Vietnamese people. And Hong Kong was supposed to welcome them all on their rest and recreation? Even my father who genuinely felt very sorry for the sailors so far from home generously invited them to our home for a drink now and again. But, I thought, leave that to the Pussycat Club girls and the Wanchai bars. Good luck to them and I hope they extort lots of money out of them and set themselves and their children up for the future.

"Why don't we go over there and have a look at it? I could take my Dad's big boat," Jimmy suddenly said. Meeli didn't want to because she got sea sick, but in the end six of us filed down to the Yacht Club pontoon and after some clambering about got on board the Alvares' family's large motor boat - and ultra luxurious it was, too. I remembered my feelings of elation and excitement, hopping around the teak deck and lying on the plush stuffed seats. The boat's captain was about to cast off but he was politely but firmly told he wasn't needed, so off we went with Jimmy at the wheel.

Jimmy revved the engine and the yacht raced across the harbour. There was a stiff breeze and all the girls shrieked when waves splashed over the bow where we were sitting and wet our hair. As we drew closer to the Enterprise we could make out a huge and gaping black hole half way up the dull grey side of the ship. It looked foreboding. The ship was so big that even at a reasonable distance it cast a dark shadow over the water.

The wind was behind us and I kept getting my hair in my face so I tied it back with the hair band I always kept on my wrist. When I raised my head after fiddling about with it I saw we were heading very fast, and directly at, the aircraft carrier. We all shouted at Jimmy to turn around before we actually hit it, when suddenly two things happened: the engine spluttered and died, and a voice through a megaphone echoed over the waves.

"This is the USS Enterprise," it bellowed. "Do not approach this ship."

Jimmy was frantically trying to get the engine started again. Tom shouted at him not to flood the damn thing. The starter motor just kept clicking fruitlessly.

"I repeat, this is the USS Enterprise. Turn around! Do not approach this ship!"

We three girls sat on a bench in the stern staring up at the ship, as our engineless yacht gaily drifted closer and closer to the aircraft carrier looming like a floating city above us. The yacht rolled slightly and swung broadside, parallel to the hole in the ship, which we could now see was some sort of enormous loading bay.

More alarmingly we could also now see twenty or so sailors running double time to the hole and lining up to face us. They were all armed and they were all pointing their guns directly at Jimmy's Dad's boat.

"Do not come any closer! This is a warning!" The stentorian megaphone shouted, somewhat pointlessly as the yacht continued to wallow and bounce in a gentle, yet relentless, approach.

"Oh for heaven's sake Jimmy, use the outboard!" screamed Loretta. He abandoned the engine and scrambled over the girls' feet to the stern of the boat. Tom and Henry, meanwhile, stood yelling back at the megaphone bearer.

"We're doing our best," they shouted, "the engine's cut out!"

"This is the USS Enterprise! This is your final warning! Turn back! Do not approach!"

"We're trying not to!" screamed Tom and Henry in unison, "can't you see? We've lost our engine!"

On board the Enterprise the sailors raised their guns to their shoulders, just as Jimmy got the little outboard going and slung the rudder round. Everybody nearly tipped out of the boat as she did a neat pirouette and suddenly had her back to the ship. Over the waves she slowly went, with all the power of her little fifteen horse-power outboard, pulling away from the massed military might of America and heading home to the cosy shambles of the Royal Hong Kong Yacht Club...

I looked out at the dull, grey sky and saw it had stopped raining. Time to get a taxi and go home to my family, I thought. It had been so great to come home unexpectedly, to phone them up and issue the delighted shock I had planned almost since I'd got to Sydney and had immediately started saving the money for my ticket home on one of Uncle Ralty's ships. When we had docked in Kowloon I'd caught the ferry over to Hong Kong side, taken a taxi to the Hilton and phoned home. Dad had answered.

"Hello Dad, it's me - Mary," I said.

He sounded a bit flummoxed. "Are you all right?"

"Yes, I'm fine. I'm at the Hilton!"

"What are you doing there?"

I was so excited I could hardly breathe, before I dropped my bombshell. "Not the Sydney Hilton Pa, at the Hong Kong Hilton!"

I heard him take a shocked breath and sit

down with a thump on the piano stool.

"Good Lord! Thel, Mary's at the Hilton! Come on, we'll go and get her! Mary, we're coming to get you, wait there!"

And I did and they did. It was wonderful to be home.

Our apartment block Peak Mansions from Mt Kellett with Mount Austin in the background with the garden at the top as described in the Easter on the Mountain story

THE VIEW FROM THE PEAK

Beside our block of flats, Peak Mansions, rose a wide path of broken tarmac edged with overgrown shrubs and weeds. It used to lead to the famous Peak Hotel. This building started life as a spectacular private house but was turned into a hotel soon afterwards, owing to its truly stunning position. It was bought and sold and extended multiple times, firstly by raising the height of the building by one or two storeys so that you could enjoy the view of the whole harbour. Then even more storeys and various annexes were added to encompass the beautiful views to the back of the island as well, over Pokfulam, the many nearby islands and the open sea beyond.

Peak Hotel was immensely popular, from its formation in 1890 until its untimely and tragic demise by a devastating fire in 1938. Apparently, it had been bought by the owners of its main rival, the Hong Kong Hotel, in 1922 and from then on allowed, or should I say, encouraged, to deteriorate until the fire finished it off – an effective way of putting your rival out of business.

For us, though, the ruins of Peak Hotel

provided a wonderful playground; a great empty space for children and dogs to roam and breathe. It was always known as "the ruins" and we spent a great deal of time exploring the mosaic floors of what must once have been verandahs, and broken, low walls defining all the different rooms, which interlinked in various different and unexpected ways, as well as finding "treasures" of all sorts, none of them valuable of course.

Two or three times a week I would walk up there. Nobody else apart from us children really bothered, certainly tourists didn't know it existed and the path didn't look at all promising, as well as giving the impression of being private. For me though, it was a retreat and a much loved place, especially as I grew older and particularly at night when I would always go by myself. I was and am very much a night person.

It would be hard to imagine a more beautiful experience than to stand alone under the stars at the top of the mountain, gazing down at the million lights of Hong Kong; the harbour sparkling with the crisscrossing of boats over the water, the glow of the myriad of Hong Kong's neon colours laid out along the whole stretch of the waterfront - and the beauty of Kowloon shining in a hundred colours right up to the deep shadows of the Nine Dragon mountains, from which the name Kowloon originates. Across the harbour the moonlight rippled constantly over the restless sea. I would stand listening to the rustle of the long grasses in the wind, and the hidden cicadas chirping endlessly, unaware of the magnificence that surrounded them.

It was often windy up on the ruins, because it was totally exposed. I would hug myself while I stood there drinking it all in. I often spoke aloud, "This is my city, my home, this is where I belong," I would say, the feeling of love and patriotism welling up until I would have to blink my eyes as it overwhelmed me.

I am aware that China has felt for a long time so much loss of face regarding having given away this benighted "barren rock", as they gleefully described it when Britain left Shanghai and was granted the island and part of Kowloon "in perpetuity". China then had to watch Hong Kong transform itself and its three fishing villages into one of the most glorious and successful cities the world has ever known.

Of course, China now wants to destroy its history. Naturally it is rewriting events and denying, amazingly, that it was ever a colony although it was ceded to Britain in 1842 at the Treaty of Nanking. In terms of new countries it was a relatively old one, founded only two years after New Zealand in 1840 and thirty years before the various warring German-speaking fiefdoms united to form a new country, Germany, in 1871.

We who lived our young lives in this colony

can never go home to it as it was; it is no longer home. We who were children and who grew to adulthood there miss it viscerally and I am in touch with quite a few. So many of us feel the loss of our home, which has left us feeling rootless and lost.

Our lives and our ways of living and thinking were formed there, this wonderful place where we were fortunate enough to grow up.

POSTSCRIPT

A STORY OF LOVE IN A BUNGALOW

Before my late, lamented husband Alan and I moved permanently to Cornwall, we used to come down from London to stay with my parents quite frequently.

They had moved from a four-bedroomed country cottage, complete with orchard and stream, to a bungalow back in Polruan. I suppose it had a lot to recommend it, mainly because it was walking distance from Mother's friends. It had a wonderful south-facing terrace with a panoramic view of the sea and it had a small field attached to it, where we as a family sometimes had afternoon parties. Mother bought a little caravan to put in the field, which became her personal Wendy house. She equipped it with frilly gingham curtains, matching cushions, plates and cutlery from Kernow Mills, all very tasteful obviously, and she had fun laying everything out for our picnics. She loved sitting on the caravan's step and watching us playing rounders, flying kites and playing games with the little grandchildren.

The downside to this idyll was the fact

that the bungalow only had two bedrooms, and their purchase of it coincided with my husband Alan's sudden and dramatic descent into Snoring World. He went from the perfect, silent, sleeping partner of over fifteen years to pneumatic drill almost exactly to the day he turned forty. Our bedroom became every light sleeper's nightmare.

Escape routes for me were limited. Mum and Dad had one sofa, about five feet long and made of slippery old leather - no point in trying to sleep on that! Also there were the dogs, who sat on the floor gazing at you and breathing their doggie breath straight into your face. If you put the sofa cushions on the floor you had to add random cushions to lengthen it. Then the dogs lay on you and your feet, sticking out at the end, froze. So Dad bought a foam fold-down sofa to solve the problem and put it in his study, where you tiptoed in trepidation so as not to disturb his music, books, batons, music stand, files, works in progress, as well as Mum's art easel and paints. When eventually you collapsed on the folded down foam bed there was an enormous piece of wood, which cut into your back and threatened to slice you in half, attached to its underside.

Lying directly on the carpet was more comfortable. Although not very much more comfortable to be honest. In fact, after a couple of hours, supremely uncomfortable. So in desperation, eventually I was often forced to go and sleep in my parents' bed.

I used to tiptoe, hollow-eyed, into their room at about two or three o'clock in the morning, and creep around to my mother's side of the bed. My parents slept noiselessly, curled in an inseparable ball together on Dad's side. They slept like this for sixty-seven years. Their bed was a standard double measuring four feet wide, but they took up so little room in it there was about a two foot slither of space for me. I would carefully lift the duvet and slide silently in. Bliss. Silence. Wow. Faintly, I could hear Alan's stentorious snoring in the other bedroom so I would smile a self-satisfied smirk and go to sleep for a little while. The mornings however, were challenging and I remember a typical one:

At about seven o'clock Mum and Dad woke up, to the sound of the useless Teasmaid dinging.

"Oh blast," whispered Dad hoarsely, "I meant to turn that off in case Mary came in."

"Don't worry Harold, she's asleep," Mum whispered back.

"Eh?"

"I said it's fine darling, she's asleep," Mum repeated more loudly.

Dad wriggled about getting himself out of bed, followed by the kerfuffle of him putting his dressing gown on and hastening to the loo, being an older man under a certain amount of pressure. Then he tottered off down the hall to the kitchen, loudly urging the dogs to follow him on the way. Once there, I could hear him filling the kettle and banging open the sticking kitchen door. I took deep, steady, sleepy-sounding breaths, not wanting Mum to be upset that they had woken me up.

Mum sat up and put on her bed jacket. (Yes, she was possibly the last known woman to wear pretty bed jackets.) She looked anxiously at me, where I lay with my eyes shut pretending to be asleep. She said a few words to herself: "Poor Mary, I hope she got a little bit of sleep," and so on, until Dad wobbled on his arthritic legs back down the hall with a pot of tea on a tray.

"I didn't bring the biscuits darling, I didn't know which you fancied?"

"I don't mind darling, any will be fine. Definitely ginger nuts though."

"Right," said Dad, slapping his knee with his characteristic gesture. Off he went again to the kitchen to get a plate of biscuits and let the dogs back in from the garden. In to the bedroom they came, panting and breathing on me. Yuck. But I continued to pretend to be asleep, because it mattered to my adorable parents that their daughter was peaceful and rested.

Almost as soon as Dad got back into bed, put the plate of biscuits down between them and started pouring the tea, the Tibbys arrived. The Tibbys were twin, completely black cats Mum had acquired at some point and they were so alike they were just called Tibby One and Tibby Two. My parents maintained they could tell them apart but I found it hard to believe and I actually caught them out once, by secretly marking a Tibby with talcum powder on his belly and they got it wrong - I maintain they did, anyway. So, the Tibbys jumped daintily onto the bed and then stood on me. They paced up and down. Then one lay about three inches from my face and started purring and kneading my hair.

"Mary must be so tired," Dad whispered, as much as whispering was possible for him, "she's very good really, she never gets cross! Look at her, sleeping away."

Mum leaned over and picked the Tibby up off me and plonked him down by the biscuits. Fastidiously and slowly, as is the way with cats, the Tibby walked with high stepping feet back onto me and lay down exactly as before. Meanwhile, the dogs were crunching ginger nuts and hobnobs. How many times had I told Mum not to feed the dogs biscuits? And every time I caught her at it she looked ludicrously guilty, like a child caught with her hand in the sweetie jar, and every single time she did it again.

The kneading, purring Tibby was being a real nuisance. I turned over, dumping him on the floor, heaving a great sigh and breathing a few heavy, sleepy breaths to reassure my parents. Immediately, the Tibby jumped up again and returned to his position with a couple of affronted mini miaouws. The more you didn't want them, the more they were there. If you felt like a cuddle the Tibbys would look at you as if you were mad.

"We mustn't wake her up," said Mum.

"I'll just put the news on very quietly," replied Dad. The bed bounced as he leaned over to the Teasmaid with its built in radio and switched it on. Immediately, a burst of Eddie Mair filled the room. The Tibby took fright, leapt over me and dashed off. At last! Hooray. Dad turned the radio up even further whilst trying to turn it down, but then he got caught up by something being discussed and, "Oh, Thel, listen to this, this is interesting!" he said, "can you hear it all right?"

"Yes darling," replied Mum, "but I thought we were going to be very quiet for Mary?"

Dad looked over at me, where I lay with my eyes closed trying not to laugh, because their efforts to keep me asleep were so funny and touching. "She's still asleep. I doubt she could hear this anyway, it's very quiet."

The radio boomed. They sipped their tea in harmony. The dogs panted. The Tibby got over his terror and returned to walk about on me. Soon, I knew they would get up, faff around getting dressed and then – bingo. They would go and have their hour-long, three-course breakfast and I could have an hour's sleep, at peace to drift off at last, safe in their love as I always have been.

The love in their bungalow lives on in my heart.

Dad at his beloved piano still composing and recording at the age of 91

APPENDIX

1. Dame Gracie Fields DBE OStJ (1898 to 1979) was an English actress, singer, comedian and star of cinema and music hall. During the 1930s she was one of the top ten film stars in Great Britain. In 1937 she was considered to be the highest paid film star in the world.

2. maid servant

3. small boats

4. a type of Chinese sailing ship with fully battened sails.

5. a person who acts as an agent for foreign organizations engaged in investment, trade, economic or political exploitation.

6. polisher

7. The Inn of the Sixth Happiness was made in 1958 by 20th Century Fox. The film was based on the true story of Gladys Aylward (1902 to 1970), a tenacious British woman, who became a missionary in China during the Second Sino-Japanese War. Directed by Mark Robson, who

received a nomination for the Academy Award for Best Director, the film stars Ingrid Bergman as Aylward and Curt Jürgens as her love interest, Captain Lin Nan, a Chinese Army officer with a Dutch father. The musical score was composed and conducted by Malcolm Arnold. The film was shot in Snowdonia, North Wales. Most of the children in the film were ethnic Chinese children from Liverpool, home to the oldest Chinese community in Europe.

8. The cicadas (/sɪˈkɑːdəz, -ˈkeɪ-/) are a superfamily, the Cicadoidea, of insects in the order Hemiptera (true bugs). They belong to the same suborder Auchenorrhyncha as smaller jumping bugs such as leafhoppers and froghoppers. The superfamily is divided into two families, the Tettigarctidae, with two species in Australia, and the Cicadidae, with more than three thousand species described from around the world; many species remain undescribed.

9. Aylward was one of three children of Thomas John Aylward and Rosina Florence, a working-class family from Edmonton, North London. From her early teens, Gladys worked as a housemaid. She was accepted by the China Inland Mission to study in a preparatory three-month course for aspiring missionaries. Due to her lack of progress in learning Chinese, she was not offered further training.

On October 15, 1930, having worked for the explorer Lieutenant Colonel Sir Francis Younghusband, she spent her life savings on a train journey to Yangcheng, Shanxi Province, China. The trip took her across Siberia on the Trans-Siberian Railway at a time when the Soviet Union and China were in an undeclared war. Detained by the Russians, she managed to escape with local help and a lift from a Japanese ship. With the help of the British Consul she then travelled across Japan where she took another ship to China.

China

Upon arriving in Yangcheng, Aylward worked with an older missionary, Jeannie Lawson, to help manage The Inn of the Eight Happinesses (八福客栈 bāfú kèzhàn in Chinese), a name based on the eight virtues of love, virtue, gentleness, tolerance, loyalty, truth, beauty and devotion. There, they provided hospitality for travellers and would also share stories about Jesus, in hope of spreading Christianity. For a time she served as an assistant to the government of the Republic of China as a foot inspector by touring the countryside to enforce the new law against footbinding of young Chinese girls. She was successful against a backdrop of much resistance and even violence at times against the inspectors.

In 1936 Aylward became a national of the

Republic of China. She took in orphans and adopted several herself. Aylward intervened in a prison riot and advocated prison reform, risking her life many times to help those in need. Two years later the region was invaded by Japanese forces and Aylward led over one hundred orphans to safety over the mountains, despite being wounded and sick, personally caring for them (and converting many to Christianity).

In 1949, when her life in China was thought to be in great danger from the Communists – the army was actively seeking out missionaries – she returned to Great Britain. Settling in Basingstoke, Hampshire she gave lectures on her work.

After her mother died, Aylward sought a return to China. After rejection by the Communist government and a stay in British-administered Hong Kong, she finally settled in Taiwan in 1958. There, she established the Gladys Aylward Orphanage where she worked until her death in 1970.

Cinematic history

A film based on Aylward's life, The Inn of the Sixth Happiness, was released in 1958. Inspired by the biography *The Small Woman* by Alan Burgess Aylward became a celebrity due to the film's popularity. She was in demand for television and media interviews. However, she was unhappy about the film which omitted her struggles. The luminous tall blonde Swedish actress Ingrid Bergman was inconsistent with Aylward's small stature, dark hair, and North London accent.

Death and legacy

Aylward died on January 3, 1970 and was buried in a small cemetery on the campus of Christ's College in Guandu, New Taipei, Taiwan. She was known to the Chinese as 艾偉德 (Ài Wěi Dé – meaning 'The Virtuous One' – a Chinese approximation to 'Aylward'). Her ministry in Taipei continues to develop and is now called Bethany Children's Home.

A London secondary school, formerly known as Weir Hall and Huxley was renamed the Gladys Aylward School shortly after her death. There is a blue commemorative plaque on the house where Gladys lived near the school at 67 Cheddington Road, London N18.

A house was also named after Gladys Aylward at Fernwood Comprehensive (formerly Secondary Modern) School, in Wollaton, Nottingham.

Numerous books, short stories, and films have been developed about the life and work of Gladys Aylward.

10. James Graham Ballard (1930 to 2009) was an English novelist, short story writer, satirist, and essayist known for provocative works of fiction

which explored the relations between human psychology, technology, sex, and mass media. In 1984, Ballard won recognition for his war novel *Empire of the Sun*, a semi-autobiographical account of a young British boy's experiences in Shanghai during Japanese occupation; the story was adapted into a 1987 film directed by Steven Spielberg. The author's journey from youth to middle-age was chronicled, with fictional inflections, in *The Kindness of Women* (1991) and in direct autobiography in *Miracles of Life* (2008). Several of his earlier works have been adapted into films, including David Cronenberg's adaptation of *Crash* (1996) and Ben Wheatley's 2015 adaptation of Ballard's 1975 novel *High-Rise*.

11. Lantau Peak or Fung Wong Shan is the second highest peak in Hong Kong and the highest point on Lantau Island, with a height of nine hundred and thirty-four metres above sea level.

12. Lloyd Triestino was a major shipping company, established in 1919 when the city of Trieste became part of Italy, after the First World War. It ran passenger services on ocean liners around the world.

13. A group which comprises multiple companies under one umbrella.

14. "Hoist with his own petard" is a phrase from a speech in William Shakespeare's play *Hamlet*. The phrase means that a bomb-maker is blown ("hoist", the past tense of "hoise") off the ground by his own bomb ("petard"), and indicates an ironic reversal or poetic justice.

15. kapok comes from the wild-harvested windfall seed pods of a majestic tree. KapoK is soft yet supportive giving a comfortable, durable, affordable option to chemically treated cotton, wool, faux latex, foams, gels and other petrochemical synthetics that mattresses are commonly made with.

16. Gweilo or gwailou is a common Cantonese slang term for Westerners. It refers to white people and has a history of racial deprecatory and pejorative use.

17. Founded and managed by the religious Cheung family, On Lok Yuen was a leading maker of ice cream, biscuits and confectionary in Hong Kong from 1920 to 1974, with its factory in Causeway Bay and its own network of restaurants. Its flagship restaurant was located at 25 to 27 Des Voeux Road, Central, where the On Lok Yuen Building still stands. To many local Chinese families in Hong Kong, On Lok Yuen was their first introduction to Western food and ice cream and On Lok Yuen was also the first ice

cream manufacturer in Hong Kong.

18. Daimaru (founded 1920) is a Japanese department store chain, principally located in the Kansai region of Japan. The chain is operated by Daimaru Matsuzakaya Department Stores, a subsidiary of J. Front Retailing. At one time Daimaru was an independent company, The Daimaru, Inc., headquartered in Chūō-ku, Osaka.

19. Maidenform Brands is a manufacturer of women's underwear, established in 1922 by seamstress Ida Rosenthal, Enid Bissett, who owned the shop that employed her and Ida's husband, William Rosenthal. They rebelled against the flat-chested designs of the time and instead produced both dresses and support undergarments, particularly bras that accentuated the natural shape of a woman's figure, hence the name Maidenform.

20. Davy Jones's Locker is an idiom for the bottom of the sea — the resting place of drowned seamen. It is used as a euphemism for death at sea (eg. to be sent to Davy Jones's Locker). Davy Jones is a nickname (used primarily by sailors) for what would be the devil of the seas.

21. A search of Google shows that Jody Nip, dancer, choreographer and dance teacher is Head Coach and Co-founder of AS Chloe School of

Gymnastics and Dance in Hong Kong...

22. Queen's Pier, named after Queen Victoria, was a public pier in front of City Hall in Edinburgh Place, Central, Hong Kong. For three generations it served not only as a public pier in day-to-day use but also as a major ceremonial arrival and departure.

23. Taoism has been connected to the philosopher Lao Tzu, who around 500 BCE (Before the Common Era) wrote the main book of Taoism, the Tao Te Ching. Taoism holds that humans and animals should live in balance with the Tao, or the universe. Taoists believe in spiritual immortality, where the spirit of the body joins the universe after death.

24. In 957 a powerful typhoon struck near Hong Kong, killing at least ten thousand people. Another powerful typhoon struck the area in 1245, killing around ten thousand people. The most severe typhoons usually occur in August and September and on October 18, 2022 Nesat reached a wind speed of up to 156 km/h.

25. wallah (plural wallahs). (India). A servant or other person responsible for something, often specified before it, for example kitchen wallah.

26. Typhoon Mary also nicknamed Bloody Mary

by the Joint Typhoon Warning Center (JTWC). It was an extremely damaging storm that was part of the 1960 Pacific typhoon season. It began as a circulation in a trough in the South China Sea. A tropical depression formed on June 2 as it was traveling clockwise. The next day it became a tropical storm and received the name Mary. It slowly moved across the sea, strengthening to a typhoon. Mary made landfall in Hong Kong on June 8, and moved through Guangdong and Fujian. Mary caused a significant amount of damage in Hong Kong and China. It was considered the worst storm to hit Hong Kong since the typhoon in 1937. The storm destroyed weak shacks made by refugees from the mainland, leaving thousands homeless. There were multiple landslides, and most of the infrastructure was damaged. More than four hundred small watercraft were either damaged or destroyed. In China, dikes and dams were damaged severely, multiple public buildings collapsed, and destroyed large swathes of farmland. Significant wind and rain was also reported in Taiwan. More than one thousand six hundred people died during the storm.

27. Shanghainese is a dialect of Wu spoken by about fourteen million people in Shanghai. There are also many Shanghainese speakers in Hong Kong. There is no standard written form of Shanghainese and it rarely appears in writing.

28. A pogrom (Russian: погро́м) is a violent riot incited with the aim of massacring or expelling an ethnic or religious group, particularly Jews.

29. Lawrence Kadoorie (1899 to 1993), Baron Kadoorie, CBE was a Hong Kong industrialist, hotelier, photographer and philanthropist.

30. Captain Mateen Ahmed Ansari GC (1916 to 1943) served in the 5th Battalion, 7th Rajput Regiment, in the Indian Army during World War II, and was a member of the British Army Aid Group. He was awarded the George Cross posthumously. The decoration, the highest British (and Commonwealth) award for bravery out of combat, was announced in a 1946 supplement to the London Gazette as being awarded for the "most conspicuous gallantry".

Ansari was taken prisoner when Japan occupied Hong Kong in December 1941, after the Battle of Hong Kong. After the Japanese discovered that he was related to the ruler of one of the Princely States they demanded that he renounce his allegiance to the British and stir up discontent in the ranks of Indian prisoners in the prison camps. He refused and was thrown into the notorious Stanley Jail in May 1942 where he was starved and brutalised. He even helped to organise escape attempts by other prisoners. Ansari was sentenced to death, with over thirty other British, Chinese and Indian prisoners and beheaded on October 29, 1943. He is buried in Stanley Military Cemetery in Hong Kong.

31. honesty before glory.

32. Sukiyaki is a Japanese dish that is prepared and served in the nabemono style. It consists of meat, which is slowly cooked or simmered at the table, alongside vegetables and other ingredients, in a shallow iron pot in a mixture of soy sauce, sugar, and mirin.

33. A traditional female hostess, entertainer and performing artist.

34. The Qingming festival or Ching Ming Festival also known as Tomb-Sweeping Day in English (sometimes also called Chinese Memorial Day, Ancestors' Day, the Clear Brightness Festival, or the Pure Brightness Festival). It is a traditional Chinese festival observed by ethnic Chinese in mainland China, Hong Kong, Macau, Taiwan, Malaysia, Singapore, Cambodia, Indonesia, Philippines, Thailand, and Vietnam. A celebration of spring, it falls on the first day of the fifth solar term (also called Qingming) of the traditional Chinese lunisolar calendar. This makes it the fifteenth day after the Spring Equinox, either April 4, 5 or 6 in a given year. During Qingming, Chinese families

visit the tombs of their ancestors to clean the gravesites and make ritual offerings to their ancestors. Offerings typically include traditional food dishes and the burning of joss sticks and joss paper. The origins of the Qingming Festival go back more than two-and-a-half thousand years, although the observance has changed significantly. In 2008 it became a public holiday in mainland China where it is associated with the consumption of qingtuan (green dumplings made of glutinous rice and Chinese mugwort or barley grass).

35. Samurai were the hereditary military nobility and officer caste of medieval and early-modern Japan from the late 12th century until their abolition in the 1870s during the Meiji era. They were the well-paid retainers of the daimyo, the great feudal landholders. Samurai had high prestige and special privileges.

36. a thick rope or cable for mooring or towing a ship.

37. The Untouchables starred Robert Stack, Walter Winchell, Nicholas Georgiade and Paul Picerni. Walter Winchell received a reported US $25,000 per episode for his narration. With his signature machine gun dialogue delivery, he could apparently rack up almost 200 words per minute!

38. In 1958 USS Enterprise (CVN-65), formerly CVA-65, now a decommissioned United States Navy aircraft carrier, was the first nuclear-powered aircraft carrier and the eighth United States naval vessel to bear the name. Like her predecessor of World War II fame, she is nicknamed "Big E".

ACKNOWLEDGEMENTS

I would like to thank Tim Saunders for his constant attention and help - and for the fact that he always answers quickly when you need him. And my sisters Trudi and Sally for being characters in my book and my life.

THE PAUL CAVE PRIZE FOR LITERATURE

The Paul Cave Prize for Literature, established
in 2023 by Tim Saunders Publications, is in
memory of Paul Astley Cave-Browne-Cave
(1917 to 2010), a hugely inspirational magazine
and book publisher. In 1960 Paul founded
Hampshire the county magazine, running
it for over 40 years. Paul was keen to help
those who had the drive and determination to
succeed, which is what this prize is all about.

What we are looking for:
All forms of poetry: haiku, free verse,
sonnet, acrostic, villanelle, ballad, limerick,
ode, elegy, flash fiction, short stories
and novellas in any genre except erotic.
Work must be new and unpublished.
International submissions welcome.

Guidelines

Poems
should not exceed 30 lines

Flash fiction
should not exceed 300 words

Short stories
should not exceed 1,000 words

Novellas
should not exceed 10,000 words

Prizes
Best Novella - £100
Best Short Story - £50
Best Flash Fiction - £25
Best Poem - £25

Winners of each category will have their
work published on this web page and
will receive a complimentary copy of The
Paul Cave Prize for Literature 2023 book
to be published by the end of 2023.

All approved submissions will feature in The
Paul Cave Prize for Literature 2023. Each writer
who submits a piece of approved work is
guaranteed to have it published in the book.

How to enter
1. email your submission(s) to
tsaunderspubs@gmail.com
2. send payment by Paypal to
tsaunderspubs@gmail.com

For more information visit:
tsaunderspubs.weebly.com

ALSO FROM TIM SAUNDERS PUBLICATIONS

Love and Death by Iain Curr
The Fourth Rising Trilogy by Tom Beardsell
Letters from Chapel Farm by Mary Buchan
That was now, this is then
by Philip Dawson-Hammond
Heathcare Heroes by Dr Mark Rickenbach
Shadows and Daisies by Sharon Webster
A Lesson in Murder by Lin Bird
Lomax at War by Dan Boylan
A Life Worth Living by Mary Cochrane
Faze by MJ White
A Dream of Destiny by DoLoraVi
Dreams Can Come True by Rebecca Mansell
The Collected Works of TA Saunders

tsaunderspubs.weebly.com

Unsolicited manuscripts welcome

ANTHOLOGIES

A Collection of Verse Vol I
Fear
A year of writing prompts 2022 to 2023
Christmas and Easter
Family and friends
Crime
Climate Change
The America Collection
Seasons
On Reflection
Collected works
Countryside
Life
Happiness
The Commonwealth Collection

tsaunderspubs.weebly.com

REGIONAL ANTHOLOGIES

The East Anglia Collection
The Hampshire Collection
The Home Counties Collection
The West Country Collection
The Northern Counties Collection
The Ireland Collection
The Wales Collection
The Scotland Collection
The East Midlands Collection
The Isle of Wight Collection

tsaunderspubs.weebly.com

CHARITY ANTHOLOGIES

Hope for Ukraine
Hope for Turkey and Syria
Hope in Disaster (for Morocco and Libya)

All royalties from our charitable anthologies
are donated to worthy causes.

tsaunderspubs.weebly.com

Mary Levycky

Mary Levycky lives with her husband Tony in Devon, England. Her family all live across the River Tamar in Cornwall and she sees them frequently.

Printed in Great Britain
by Amazon

58091949R00179